Imagination: A Very Short Introduction

VERY SHORT INTRODUCTIONS are for anyone wanting a stimulating and accessible way into a new subject. They are written by experts, and have been translated into more than 45 different languages.

The series began in 1995, and now covers a wide variety of topics in every discipline. The VSI library currently contains over 700 volumes—a Very Short Introduction to everything from Psychology and Philosophy of Science to American History and Relativity—and continues to grow in every subject area.

Very Short Introductions available now:

ABOLITIONISM Richard S. Newman
THE ABRAHAMIC RELIGIONS Charles L. Cohen
ACCOUNTING Christopher Nobes
ADDICTION Keith Humphreys
ADOLESCENCE Peter K. Smith
THEODOR W. ADORNO Andrew Bowie
ADVERTISING Winston Fletcher
AERIAL WARFARE Frank Ledwidge
AESTHETICS Bence Nanay
AFRICAN AMERICAN HISTORY Jonathan Scott Holloway
AFRICAN AMERICAN RELIGION Eddie S. Glaude Jr
AFRICAN HISTORY John Parker and Richard Rathbone
AFRICAN POLITICS Ian Taylor
AFRICAN RELIGIONS Jacob K. Olupona
AGEING Nancy A. Pachana
AGNOSTICISM Robin Le Poidevin
AGRICULTURE Paul Brassley and Richard Soffe
ALEXANDER THE GREAT Hugh Bowden
ALGEBRA Peter M. Higgins
AMERICAN BUSINESS HISTORY Walter A. Friedman
AMERICAN CULTURAL HISTORY Eric Avila
AMERICAN FOREIGN RELATIONS Andrew Preston
AMERICAN HISTORY Paul S. Boyer
AMERICAN IMMIGRATION David A. Gerber
AMERICAN INTELLECTUAL HISTORY Jennifer Ratner-Rosenhagen
THE AMERICAN JUDICIAL SYSTEM Charles L. Zelden
AMERICAN LEGAL HISTORY G. Edward White
AMERICAN MILITARY HISTORY Joseph T. Glatthaar
AMERICAN NAVAL HISTORY Craig L. Symonds
AMERICAN POETRY David Caplan
AMERICAN POLITICAL HISTORY Donald Critchlow
AMERICAN POLITICAL PARTIES AND ELECTIONS L. Sandy Maisel
AMERICAN POLITICS Richard M. Valelly
THE AMERICAN PRESIDENCY Charles O. Jones
THE AMERICAN REVOLUTION Robert J. Allison
AMERICAN SLAVERY Heather Andrea Williams
THE AMERICAN SOUTH Charles Reagan Wilson
THE AMERICAN WEST Stephen Aron
AMERICAN WOMEN'S HISTORY Susan Ware
AMPHIBIANS T. S. Kemp
ANAESTHESIA Aidan O'Donnell

*For Steve Magill*

# Contents

# List of illustrations

# Chapter 1
# What is imagination?

The ability for human beings to imagine is virtually unlimited, for through imagining we can mentally engage ideas unconstrained by reality. Imagination's exercise allows for an escape from, without ever leaving, our ordinary life. Yet imagination also endows our lives with possibility. While we cannot intervene in reality simply by imagining it otherwise, we can regard it in a new light. Endowed by imagination, we can press beyond existing constraints and realize the transformation of a given state of things. This book is dedicated to exploring imagination and its importance in human thought and experience. It draws from philosophy, the human sciences, and literary theory. It attends to examples of imagination across ancient and modern human cultures—from art, science, literature, music, and everyday life—in order to demonstrate the reach and depth of its contributions.

This first chapter will be devoted to defining imagination, accounting for the variety of imaginative experience and the ways imagination tends to elude understanding. In the second chapter we will consider the evolution of imagination and its contribution to the emergence of human culture. In Chapters 3, 4, and 5, we will examine philosophies of imagination from the ancients to the 20th century in order to grasp imagination's roles in human thinking. These include imagination's deviation from as well as participation in knowledge, its association with madness, its role in poetry and art and in thinking possibilities, its ties to emotions, its role in perception, its relation to beauty, the sublime, and tragedy, to our sense of the transcendent and human freedom, and its ways of augmenting our sense of reality. As the expressive manifestation of imaginative thinking and being, creativity is an important theme throughout this book, but the final chapter takes a closer look at creativity and its support for human flourishing.

## The value and variety of imaginative experience

Imagination is wide-ranging, and distinguishes human life in countless ways. In order to understand imagination, we must first recognize just how varied are its contributions to our experience. Imagination is the medium of children's pretend play and an audience's absorption in a drama. Imagination consoles mourners with visions beyond earthly life. Artists depict life from novel perspectives, crafting imagined worlds for readers to virtually inhabit. Imagination is responsible for innovation. The invention of the kite in ancient China, the design of the Egyptian pyramids, the moon landing, and advancement in medical technology are all indebted to human imagining among other cognitive skills.

Imagination is, of course, also the medium of fantasies and daydreams. Children may dream of being able to fly, or of having superhero strength, and they interweave their fantasies into play. Adults too entertain unlikely scenarios—becoming a champion boxer or figure skater, winning the lottery—or impossible ones—evading mortality. To imagination, it matters not how vanishing or nil these prospects may be in real life. Imagination can stake claims well beyond the probable or even possible.

Apart from fantasy, our grasp of reality itself owes much to imagination. We can start with our grasp of the past. An understanding of history might be dry and far less vivid, even incomplete, if we had no means to place knowledge into some experiential context. In accordance with known facts, yet going beyond the strictly known, we can imagine what it might have been like to live as a soldier in ancient Sparta, or as a scribe in medieval Italy, or to have been present at the signing of the Declaration of Independence. Culture is in many senses an inheritance of imagination.

Even literary narratives may bring historical events and places to life by imagining fictional characters in the midst of them. While we would not look to Leo Tolstoy's novel *War and Peace* (1869) for historical evidence about 19th-century Russia, the novel can help us to imagine its culture under the impact of the Napoleonic wars. In her novel *Jazz* (1992) the American Nobel laureate Toni Morrison, combining historical research with the force of her imagination, brought the Harlem Renaissance and the American South of the turn of the 20th century to life for those born long after.

With the help of imaginative works, we can also think across different perspectives within our own time. Putting ourselves 'in another person's shoes', we take up an imagined point of view. Through imagination, we can try to come to a better understanding of those different from ourselves. When we fail in such imagining, differences may seem more insurmountable than they are. Imagination thus plays an important role in ethical and political life.

Imagination also plays with time. We do not simply remember the past but may see it in a new light. Mistakes made can be imagined undone, in the mind. While this may feed regret, such reflection can also help us to learn from past error. Through imagining alternatives to it, we can reflect on the present. We can envision other possible ways to live in the here and now, and project future goals for which to aim.

Given such tremendous flexibility, imagination has been revered for its expansion of human life and its contributions to human achievement. Yet imagination has also been blamed for disturbances in our sense of reality. Distracted by inflated imagining, we can submit to false hopes. Imagination may inflame emotions, sustain outsized anxieties and fears. Imagination is the currency of conspiracy theories and when combined with cultural anxieties it can feed prejudice. While imagination is widely celebrated in popular culture today, it was castigated throughout history for confounding fantasy and perception, illusion and reality.

The attack on imagination goes all the way back to Plato. Despite being an exceptionally imaginative philosopher himself, in his *Republic* (*c.*375 BCE), Plato maligned imagination as the medium of error and confusion. In the 17th century the French mathematician and philosopher Blaise Pascal declared imagination the very 'enemy of reason'. In his *Pensées* (1660), Pascal described imagination as 'that deceitful part in man [*sic*], that mistress of error and falsity, the more deceptive that she [*sic*] is not always so'. Being 'generally false', Pascal thought, imagination 'cannot set a true value on things'. In his novel *Rasselas* (1759), the British writer Samuel Johnson deemed imagination depraved, seducing the mind to feast on 'luscious falsehood' whenever 'offended with the bitterness of truth'. Imaginative indulgence is there illustrated by the character of a mad astronomer who believes himself in 'imaginary dominion' over the weather, dispensing sunshine and rain around the globe at will. In recent decades, psychologists have investigated imagination's potential to distort memories, or, controversially, to mix the feeling of remembrance with ideas imagined rather than recalled.

As imagination's product, literature and art have been criticized for tarrying with illusion or cultivating irrational passions. Plato worried that the arts, in particular dramatic and epic poetry, would miseducate citizens, disrupting social order. Johnson warned that the luxuries of fiction would turn the mind to reject the 'insipidity of truth'. The Spanish writer Miguel de Cervantes rendered the protagonist of *Don Quixote* (1605) a ridiculous figure by way of the overinfluence of imaginative literature. The self-proclaimed knight, having read too many chivalrous tales, casts his fantastical eye everywhere and sees the world as he imagines it. Quixote fights windmills he imagines are really giants disguised as windmills. The irony of Cervantes' treatment is of course that his own reader too is indulging in an imagined world.

Against the tide of criticism, other philosophers recognized imagination as an enhancement of the human mind. Departing from his teacher Plato, Aristotle argued that all thinking requires imagination. The mind never thinks without an image, he claimed; images—one of the main currencies of imagination—are the very stuff of thought. In his treatment of dramatic poetry, Aristotle praised the capacity to think possibilities, enabling understanding not only of what has happened, but of what *could* happen. This appreciation will be echoed in the 18th century with the German philosopher Immanuel Kant and the rise of aesthetics. The idea of the productive imagination to which the thinking of possibility is attributed will be rapturously elaborated by Romantic writers.

Since the 19th century, as scientific thinking came to be regarded a culture apart from or even opposed to the humanities and arts, literary writers have been imagination's staunch defenders. The American poet Wallace Stevens hailed imagination as the power of the mind to grasp the possibilities of things. Imagination, he wrote in *The Necessary Angel: Essays on Reality and Imagination*, relieves the 'pressure of reality' by creating other perspectives for our minds to consider. The Irish Nobel laureate Seamus Heaney described in 'The Redress of Poetry' how imagination enables us to respond variably to misfortune, allowing us to recognize the nature of our predicament and consider possible redress—'tilting the scales of reality towards some transcendent equilibrium'.

Because of this, Heaney claims, imagination 'has a liberating and verifying effect upon the individual spirit'.

It may be perplexing to think that the very same capacity that allows us to evade the pressure of reality, or can confuse us about it, may be required to understand it. Scientific discovery, however, owes much to imagination. Famously praising imagination as 'more important' than knowledge, Albert Einstein detailed his own use of imagination in achieving discoveries in physics that revolutionized our understanding of space and time. Einstein described processes of inner visualization through which he conjured hypothetical scenarios against which to test existing knowledge. Einstein described inspiration while playing the violin, such that ideas arose as images in his mind before being expressed in language and scientific concepts.



Einstein's own imagination may be considered a special case of genius. Yet he himself thought that imagination was required for all scientific progress. He wrote in *The Evolution of Physics* (1938) that: 'To raise new questions, new possibilities, to regard old problems from a new angle, requires creative imagination and marks real advance in science.' Other scientists have echoed Einstein's appraisal of imagination. Nobel laureates for physiology or medicine François Jacob (1965) and Eric R. Kandel (2000) have written eloquently about the close analogy between scientific enquiry and artistic creation, while Elizabeth Blackburn (2009) described as beautiful 'the very process of scientific inquiry by which human creativity and ingenuity unveil a pattern within what had looked like chaos and incomprehensibility'. Whether or not imagination is more important than knowledge, scientists have argued that existing knowledge cannot evolve without it.

We have so far described how imagination allows us to escape reality, distorts our sense of it, allows us to take a new perspective on it, and even to understand it. From play and dreams to art and science, imagining is central to many human experiences and accomplishments. Does imagination work differently across these different kinds of experiences? Are we really speaking of one and the same facility, or are these experiences manifesting a variety of mental capacities? In the rest of this chapter we will address some challenges in defining imagination and identify its multiple modes.

## The elusiveness of imagination

Imagination, which has so deeply influenced human history, has not been well understood for much of it. Even philosophers who assigned imagination a significant role in their theories of the mind admitted that understanding imagination is a daunting challenge. The British philosopher David Hume described imagination eluding philosophy's grasp, as a 'kind of magical faculty' which is 'inexplicable by the utmost efforts of human understanding'. Kant called imagination 'a hidden art in the depths of the human soul, whose true operations we can divine from nature and lay unveiled before our eyes only with difficulty'. Yet we can get closer to defining imagination by identifying those very characteristics which render it so elusive.



The first such characteristic is the *heterogeneity* of the concept. By 'imagining' we may mean conjuring something like a visual image in our minds, as we may do in fantasizing or daydreaming. Inner images comprise much of what we often refer to as the content of imagining. Or we may mean considering other possibilities than the current situation, without any inner imaging at all. We have mentioned forms of creativity and invention, pretending and play, all of which engage imagination. Some of these are experiential in nature, involving something akin to inner perception, while others are conceptual in nature. Some of these take place wholly in the individual mind, while others arise through social or material interaction.

Imagination is most typically identified in the history of philosophy as inner representation of what is not present to perception. Imagining in this sense draws up a mental image or other schematic representation on the basis of previous experience. The French philosopher René Descartes, for example, treated the imagination as a kind of mental envisioning. He illustrated this faculty by pointing out that while he could imagine or inwardly 'picture' a triangle with its three sides, he could only conceptualize, but not imagine, a thousand-sided figure. This mode of imagining has been said to take place in 'the mind's eye' and involves a quasi-visual experience. Apart from sight, inner presentations of imagination could invoke other senses, such as the sound of a whistle, or the taste of a lemon, or the feel of silk.

Other philosophers have regarded imagination not principally as inner envisioning but as a form of pretence. Pretence can be taken to encompass the ability to entertain counterfactual scenarios, such as my imagining that I am a farmer in ancient Mesopotamia, rather than at my desk typing these words as I am doing here and now. Or one may take something present as a stand-in for something not present, as children at play could pretend that the log is a pirate ship and a meadow the surrounding sea. Pretence could involve the experiential component of inward visualization or other imaging of the same, but it could also be conceived as strictly conceptual.



A strictly conceptual or 'propositional' view of imagination as pretence was defended by the British philosopher Gilbert Ryle in his influential work *The Concept of Mind* (1949). In Ryle's oft-cited example, I can imagine a nursery from my childhood. For Ryle such imagining means that I only need pretend, or imagine *that*, I am seeing the room. No inner visual experience, nothing like an inner image of this room, need be present in my mind. Since inner images are unnecessary for imagining to occur, Ryle argued, they are not an essential part of imagination.

This view, however, has been countered by examples of imagining for which visualization is essential. Without any fruits at hand, comparing the yellow of a banana to that of a lemon, for example, will require something like an inner envisioning of it. Moreover, in imagining a childhood room, both pretence and an attending quasi-visualization may be involved: while I 'pretend' that I see a room of my childhood home, I may also experience something like a visual image of such a room, which for many imaginers would be felt to fulfil the experience of truly imagining it. The debate between proponents of propositional imagination and those of experiential imagination reflects different models of the mind, and may reflect, as William James pointed out in *Principles of Psychology* over a century ago, variation in imaginers' capacities for inner visualization. We can get around this impasse if we understand imagination not as a single faculty but as heterogeneous, admitting multiple modes. Before addressing these, we can consider further difficulties imagination poses to any reductive explication.

A characteristic of imagination is its *variability in relation to our will*. We can sometimes deliberately imagine as we wish to. We can gaze at the clouds and identify the shapes they might make. We can, writing a short story, compose what will happen next. We can come up with a joke to introduce a speech. Alternatively, our will to imagine can fail. We can try to conjure an image of something without succeeding, or try to come up with a new idea, but fall short.

Yet we can also imagine more passively. Dreaming involves imagination wholly passive to the will. In daydreaming, imagined ideas may simply appear in the flow of our awareness, as if of their own accord, untethered to our current reality. Without effort or direction, the clouds may suddenly appear to us in the shape of a face, or an animal. The boundary between deliberate imagining and its unwilled flow in fantasizing may be blurred in creativity, where a receptive flow of ideas can be channelled towards elaboration. In such experience it may be difficult to discern any clear boundary between our willed exertion of imagination and passive imagining.

A third feature of imagination that renders it elusive to observation is its *introspective nature*. While imagination may be outwardly expressed, the process of imagining itself cannot be directly observed by others. What I am imagining may be wholly invisible and inaccessible to you, and vice versa. While we can scan the brain of an imagining subject to observe an imaginer's areas of neuronal activity, imagining occurs from the first-person perspective, and cannot be fully understood in isolation from this.

For this reason, phenomenology is often enlisted in efforts to understand imagination. Phenomenology is the study, from a first-person perspective, of what appears to consciousness and the structure this takes. While a formal philosophical method invented at the turn of the 20th century by the philosopher Edmund Husserl, phenomenology can be engaged informally whenever we reflect on and describe our first-person lived experience. French phenomenological philosophers such as Jean-Paul Sartre, Maurice Merleau-Ponty, and Paul Ricoeur dedicated phenomenological studies to imagination and its processes, as we will see in Chapter 5.

A fourth and final difficulty that needs to be mentioned is *the term 'imagination' itself*. Its multiplicity also helps to explain some of the complexity of the conceptual history of imagination—the way over time imagination as a concept has been defined and examined. While the reader of this book can make do without keeping in mind the following distinctions, familiarity with the etymological multiplicity of the term may help to avoid potential confusions as we go along. The word *imagination*, along with *image*, *imaginary*, *imaginative*, and so on, is derived from Latin. In Latin *imago* means 'image' and *imaginari* means 'to picture to oneself'. Yet we also use the term *fantasy*, along with *fantastical*, *fancy*, and so on, derived from Greek. *Phantasia* in ancient Greek means the perception of appearances or bringing an object to mind in its absence to perception. While in English *imagination* and *fantasy* are often used interchangeably, they are occasionally distinguished. *Fantasy* or *fancy* is sometimes used, as for instance by Shakespeare, when the illusory quality of ideas is emphasized. Yet other writers, such as Samuel Johnson, do not distinguish always between imagination and fancy, regarding imagination itself in light of the vulnerabilities of illusory thinking.

German-language philosophers use several terms which we translate as 'imagination'. In addition to the borrowed *die Imagination* or *die Phantasie*, we find *Einbildungskraft*, which for Kant involves making an image (*Bild*) from diverse sense-impressions. Also translated into 'imagination' is *Vorstellungskraft*, the power to represent, used both by Kant and by the Austrian philosopher Ludwig Wittgenstein. Prominent in Husserl's discussions is also the term *Vergegenwärtigung*, presentifying or making-present to consciousness, a task ascribed to imagination.



## Reproductive and productive imagination

We have so far identified imagination as an activity of consciousness, whether wilfully directed or passively experienced, that presents images or ideas of what is not immediately given in perception, and may potentially transform them. Such presentation and transformation may happen in the mind alone, or also through material or linguistic creativity. Imagination thus defined admits of multiple modes. Before identifying these, we must make a further distinction.

Crucial to understanding the scope of imagination's involvement in human cognition is the distinction between reproductive and productive imagination. With reproductive imagination, we call up or conjure in the mind images or ideas we already know from past perceptions or experiences. Aristotle thus classed imagination of this kind as a form of memory. Yet what we so imagine is not strictly speaking only a reproduction of memory. If we remember a particular car we once drove or an elephant with which we spent time at a sanctuary, for example, the memory will be specific to what was once perceived. Yet we can also imagine a car or an elephant without it representing any specific vehicle or animal. In this case we may draw from various memories while generating a schema that abstracts from any particular experience.

Reproductive imaginings can be altered or combined to make a new image. We can imagine a car and an elephant. We can imagine an elephant inside a car. We can further imagine an elephant driving a car. Here the new idea clearly exceeds any original ingredients previous experience could have provided. This new idea may provoke still further elaborations, for example, in writing a children's book or drawing a political cartoon. Many accounts of imagination that describe such combination or synthesis regard imagination as an entirely reproductive function. Yet sometimes we are able to imagine in ways that produce new ideas, the meaning of which cannot be wholly accounted for by adding up old ones.



We can find an example in literature. Shakespeare relied on previous experience and knowledge when he wrote his play *Hamlet*, in which the protagonist considers how to react to his uncle's (purported) murder of his father, the king. The author would have had knowledge of princes, of political intrigue, of patricides and regicides, and even of a similar name, Hamnet, that of his own son. Shakespeare would have had some knowledge from life, history, or existing drama of human psychology. To claim, however, that the character Hamlet is only an amalgamation of previous ideas held by Shakespeare would not capture the novelty of his creation. The particular character of the inner life—or as Shakespeare puts it, 'that within'—constructed by

Hamlet's indecisive brooding is among the qualities newly introduced by Shakespeare's dramatic fiction.

Beyond such novelty, productive imagination may have a further, more fundamental role in thinking. Rather than only producing novel ideas, productive imagination may generate the very shape of experience. As we will see in more detail in Chapter 3, Kant thought that imagination was involved in generating the structure of human perception itself. Kant argued that, among other roles imagination performs, imagination in its productive use synthesizes sensation into a coherent image, so that we are able to perceive complex sensory objects that remain constant across successive moments of perception. Since imagination mediates between other faculties (for Kant these are sensibility and understanding), Kant called this activity of productive imagination 'transcendental'. More recently, cognitive theorists ascribe to imagination a similarly productive role in that it is said to constantly blend concepts to form new ones. In this role imagination is held to work in the background of our awareness such that it is inaccessible to observation.



A more accessible example of productive imagination offered by Kant can be found in the aesthetic experience of beauty. When we perceive a sunset or an orchid as beautiful, we do not merely register its empirical details, or regard it in conceptual terms. We do not see in the sunset only a scattering of light rays, or in the orchid just a part of a plant with a reproductive function. We also feel enlivened by the harmony or vitality of what is perceived, by its beauty or other striking aesthetic quality, which, according to Kant, provokes a free play of imagination with another faculty of the mind, the understanding. When something strikes us as beautiful, Kant suggests, we are perceiving it through the play of imagination.

This aesthetic effect is due not to the features of the object alone, but rather to the activities of the perceiving subject that these features stimulate. To put it another way, for Kant beauty is not so much in the eye as in the imagination of the beholder—or rather in imagination's play with the faculty of understanding. Sartre too recognized the beauty of a landscape as indebted to the consciousness which beholds it. For the mind configures relations among this and that element, holds the multiplicity in a harmonious or striking configuration. It is consciousness that lends qualities to regard the landscape as majestic or serene. In these ways we might say that imagination is productive, generating an interpretive perspective through which the world is revealed in a certain way.

So far, we have suggested that imagination is active in a wide range of human experiences. Imagination is an activity of consciousness that can be directed or passive, or some combination of these. It can engage ideas reproductively or also productively contribute to shaping experience. We can now consider some major modes of imagining.



## Modes of imagining

The activity of imagining can be undertaken in several modes. These include inner imaging, including visual or other sense presentation in the mind; pretence, and closely related to that, hypothetical or counterfactual thinking; concrete imagining or 'seeing-as'; and creativity. Many philosophers have focused on one of these capacities alone as paradigmatic of imagining. While such approaches enable a more streamlined analysis, a multimodal view of imagination can register both its range and the depths of its involvement in human thinking.

Inner visualization and other inner imaging comprise the most frequently discussed mode of imaginative activity. It is the subject of Sartre's phenomenological analysis in *The Imaginary* (1940) and more recently of empirical study in psychology. Yet inner visualization is accessible to most people through reflection, as long as they have had the experience of closing their eyes and drawing to their 'mind's eye' something like a visual image.

For example, I can image a snowman, even if it is a hot summer day. Something that was not there already in my mind, and is not there to my immediate perception, is presented and appears in my thought. Such imagining enables us to think freely untethered to perception. Beyond presentation, imagination can also transform such an image. I can imagine the snowman on a beach, wiping its melting forehead with a handkerchief. Drawn schematically on the basis of memories, such inner phenomena have a visual quality even if they are not exactly pictures in the mind.

Inner imaging is not only visual in nature, however, but may involve any of the senses. I can similarly evoke sounds, smells, tastes, or tactile sensations. Beyond the five senses, I can evoke kinaesthetic feelings, or sensations of movement, such as falling, floating, or running fast. I can also imagine proprioceptive sensation: hunger, or pain, or being out of breath. While inner imaging is often described in visual terms, it can evoke multiple sensations of embodied experience.



Pretence is not limited to pretending, but can encompass entertainment of a counterfactual idea, hypothetical thinking, and taking one thing as a stand-in for another. As in Ryle's example of imagining that I see my childhood room, I can imagine that something is the case (when it is not). I can imagine that I am Napoleon Bonaparte, and wonder how I might feel in captivity on the island of Saint Helena. Counterfactual imagining can also be intertwined with hypothetical thinking (as in, if *this* is supposed, then *that* could follow). I can imagine that I have won the lottery, and consider various prospects as if I were in the position to distribute the winnings. Pretence also allows us to 'take *this* for *that*'—as in our earlier example, taking a log for a pirate ship. This same capacity allows us to become immersed in the fictional situations of theatre and drama, to take that particular actor for

Hamlet, and the theatre stage for the room of a medieval castle in Denmark. Taking one thing for another is the basis of metaphoric and symbolic thinking. Thus pretence has been described as the origin of the arts.

Concrete imagining, aspect perception, or 'seeing-as', all describe that mode of imagining which is dependent upon perception, yet generates meaning, resemblance, or value beyond what is directly given perceptually. Seeing faces in the clouds is an example of 'seeing-as', also called 'seeing an aspect' or aspect perception, explored by Wittgenstein, who recognized in such phenomena the involvement of imagination in perception. The related phenomenon of 'concrete' imaging was described by Sartre as seeing in perceived objects some symbolic value or quality. We have mentioned the beautiful landscape that may be seen as majestic or serene. Through imagination, Sartre says, we lend our emotion to perceptual phenomena and perceive more than what is empirically present. This augmentation in our perception of reality will be discussed in more detail in Chapters 2 and 5.



Inner imaging, pretence, and 'seeing-as' are all presentational activities of consciousness in which what is presented—an image or idea or a proposition or an evoked experience—is undetermined by present perception. These presentations are all malleable in ways our perception of reality is not, and thus they are all latently or actively transformative. Creativity involves any of these modes of imagination becoming expressive, playing and working with the media of language, images, sounds, bodily movement, or physical matter. We will devote the final chapter of this book to considering creativity in more detail, while many endeavours of human creativity will serve as examples throughout.

Imagination is wide-ranging in scope and significance for human life, playing a crucial role in consciousness and admitting multiple modes. Imagining allows us to step back from our immediate perceptions or thoughts and entertain and elaborate possibilities.

Visualizing or other inner imaging, pretending or entertaining other states of affairs, conceiving counterfactual or hypothetical possibilities, and seeing things in symbolical ways or as latent with meaning all allow us to take a stance towards the world, to develop a perspective on it, and potentially to transform it.

Imagining otherwise than what is merely given, we can respond to it more freely. Engaging imagination, we can creatively express new ideas and sometimes integrate them in reality. In the next chapter we will explore the emergence of imagination in human evolution and its role in the emergence of human culture.

# Chapter 2
# Imagination in human evolution

Imagination has nurtured human thinking for around 50,000 years and has distinguished our species as the most innovative on the planet. As our early human ancestors adapted to changing environments, established social groups, and developed more complex ways of ensuring their survival, they began to create decorative works and to represent their world in novel ways. Evidence of tool and body decorations, sculptures, cave paintings, burial rituals, and toys made by prehistoric humans suggests a gradually evolving capacity for imaginative thought and creativity. In order to grasp how imagination emerged, it is necessary to consider human consciousness itself not as separated from the surrounding world but as evolving in interaction with it.

Approaching imagination as an evolved dimension of human consciousness requires complementing philosophical understanding with insights from other disciplines. While the dominant model of the mind in modern philosophy essentially divided it from the body, phenomenology and contemporary philosophies of mind have acknowledged its embodied and enactive nature. This means that the capacity for us to think about the world emerges through our physical and psychological involvement with it, and that the world's meaning for us emerges through our interactive concerns. Along with philosophy, knowledge of prehistoric artefacts, of early human groups and their migrations, of the psychological development of modern human children, and of primate cognition have all been enlisted to help explain how imagination may have evolved in early human interaction with the world.

## Evolving imagination

Imagination is a relatively recent development in evolution. From about 5 million years ago up to the emergence of the first member of our genus, our pre-human ancestors came to walk on two legs, make rudimentary hand tools from stone, and develop in brain size due to the increased consumption of protein. From the appearance of *Homo ergaster* 1.9 million years ago, early humans would have developed new cognitive capacities through further tool-making, migration, and planned hunting. From half a million years to 100,000 ago, *Homo neanderthalensis* in Europe and pre-human ancestors in Africa developed again dramatically in brain size and in technical and communication skills. Around 200,000 years ago modern *Homo sapiens* emerged in Africa and by 60,000 years ago had wandered into Eurasia. Around this time—around 50,000 years ago—new ways of thinking emerged among our early human ancestors.



While less developed than early *Homo sapiens*, their Neanderthal relatives left evidence of bodily decoration, ornament-making, burials of their dead, and, around 41,000 years ago, simple cave paintings with red dots, lines, and hand stencils on cave walls. Yet Neanderthals were to be surpassed, and by about 40,000 years ago, *Homo sapiens* remained the only human species left. They engaged in more complex social organization, travelled further in search of food, and made more advanced decorative works. Their representations of animals and other living beings gradually expanded to include expressive and symbolic depictions, giving rise to the capacity for myth and fictionalization.

It is widely argued that the capacity for imagination was enhanced with the migrations of early humans in search of food. As early humans took in the view of surrounding lands from a distance, perhaps climbing hills to get a view from above, they would have been able to consider the landscape from new and variable perspectives. This would have conferred tactical advantages, supporting the planning of hunts or mapping out new territory. The comparison of different perspectives may have also enabled the gradual emergence of representational skills and exercised cognition of possibilities.

Imaginative capacities would have also developed in correlation with specific practical skills. One example is the development of projectile tools, such as javelins, that require aiming a throw. Chimpanzees and other monkeys do throw objects in displays of aggression and some can anticipate the trajectory of objects that are thrown towards them. Yet aimed throwing at a moving target is a skill other species do not appear to be able to do with accuracy. The earliest known projectile tools early humans used for this purpose were made 280,000 years ago in Ethiopia. It has been argued that the mind's capacity for internal representation was gradually enabled by the repeated actions of aiming a spear or other projectile at moving prey.

On this theory, the process of aiming one object at another moving object may promote a special cognitive function. During the process of an aimed throw, neural feedback generates anticipatory calculations. This cognitive process is thought to have given rise to inner visual schemata, as the thrower simulates inwardly where the moving target may be next. Along with memory and other material interactions with their environment, this may have provided early humans with a cognitive basis for a mode of imagination, that of inner mental imaging or representation.

Moreover, the availability of such tools would have allowed early humans to be able to plan their activities. It would have been advantageous to be able to consider and even represent prospective strategies for hunting before taking risks to implement them, thus stimulating hypothetical thinking. Tools were also among the first objects of decoration. Both the comparative contemplation of possibilities and the decorative embellishment occasioned by tools would have supported the development of imaginative thought.

Early cave painters and carvers not only represented animals and other living beings they observed in the world around them. They also reconfigured their representations to transform their subject matter. The earliest known symbolic artefact and sculpture was made around 40,000 years ago, when a prehistoric carver made a half-human, half-lion figurine around 30 centimetres tall from a mammoth tusk. Found in the Hohlenstein-Stadel in Germany, the zoomorphic lion-man figure manifests the emergence of creative imagination, and perhaps the first evidence of fictional thought (Figure 1).

Perhaps the most widely recognized prehistoric artworks are the Palaeolithic cave paintings of Lascaux, France. Until their rediscovery in 1940 they had been sealed from view for around 17,000 years since they had been created. On the walls of the chambers were preserved thousands of paintings, drawings, and carvings. We can now view a splendorous array of bison, horses, deer, birds, mammoths, bears, wolves, felines, aurochs, and other animals, with the polychromatic paintings in red, yellow, ochre, violet, brown, and black mineral pigments.

What is now known as the Lascaux Shaft scene is particularly significant, despite the fact that its monochrome black oxide, painted over a natural protrusion in a wall, is at first glance less visually striking than the polychromatic works. Yet the scene presents the only rendering of a human figure in the cave complex, albeit one fantastically imagined. A man appears with the head of a bird—or in a bird mask—and only four fingers on each hand,

1. The Löwenmensch, or 'Lion-Man', an ivory sculpture between 35,000 and 41,000 years old, discovered in Hohlenstein-Stadel in 1939.

perhaps suggesting an animalistic being of mythic significance. The bird-man is lying prostrate and appears to be dying at the feet of a wounded bison (its entrails are hanging down) which has turned to gouge the hunter. Nearby is a goose or other bird at the end of a staff. A few feet away is the outline of what appears to be a woolly rhinoceros.

It has been suggested that this fantastical rendering of the bird-man figure could represent ancestors of the group to which the painter belonged; magic rituals around hunting; a burial marking for a slain hunter; or a spiritual vision. The work has also been interpreted as shamanic cosmology, in that the three points of the man, bison, and bird appear to repeat the asterism, or pattern of stars, in the northern celestial hemisphere called the Summer Triangle. Another theory is that the Lascaux Shaft scene may have recorded a cosmic event, the death of the bird-man and bison representing a catastrophic comet strike at Lascaux around 15200 BCE. Whatever meaning it had to its creator, the scene combines realistic, symbolic, and mythical elements, and yields fascinating early evidence of the productive imagination.

## Seeing-as and the early human view of the world

Along with inner representation and hypothetical thinking, human cognitive evolution saw the emergence of our capacity for 'seeing-as'. This facility describes the way in which through visual perception we may perceive in one thing or group of things the shape of another: while I perceive the clouds above as white moving puffs against the sky, I may sometimes 'see' in them familiar objects, such as a face or a turtle. This embellishment may be ascribed in part to the fact that recognizing patterns or figures is a strength of the human visual system. The human eye and brain register and visually categorize faces and animals through faster neural pathways than those which process visual detail. The visual recognition of faces would have enabled social bonding, while that of animal bodies, the evasion of threats or the pursuit of food.

Such facility may influence the perception of patterns or figures in other objects and is thought to have spilled over into the making of early human art.

Cave paintings, for example, suggest the recognition of figures in the shapes of natural surfaces, evidencing imagination's involvement with sensory perception. On the Chauvet cave in France, where hundreds of representational paintings of deer, lions, rhinoceros, and other animals were made around 36,000 years ago, a bear's head can be seen painted on a natural protrusion. The relief of the rock wall is suggestive of the bear head painted in outline, and the circular indication of an eye was placed in its anatomically appropriate location by the painter. Along with the bears then present in the area, the shape of the protrusion may have prompted the idea for the painting.



This capacity for seeing-as, likely to have enhanced early human thinking, persists as a function of the modern human artistic mind. Seeing-as would be practised deliberately by artists of the Renaissance. Leonardo da Vinci looked for patterns everywhere in nature. The master advised his students to find images of humans, animals, and scenes in natural figurations, even in the settling of dust on a surface. His younger rival Michelangelo similarly engaged in interpretive perception, seeing his subject matter in the stone that was to become his sculpture. He reportedly claimed that he saw a statue in every block of marble, and he needed only to chisel away what did not belong in order to liberate it from the stone.

In seeing-as, one thing is perceptually interpreted as another through partial resemblance. In a similar process one object can also serve as or stand in for another. Wittgenstein offered among his examples of seeing-as that of seeing a triangle on its side as a mountain. With only rudimentary perceptual resemblance (its basic shape), the perception becomes symbolic, and can enable analogical thinking. To recognize geographical features on a map, for example, the viewer grasps resemblance to what a given mark stands for, in respect to other features in the respective visual frameworks. On the map the curved line is to the triangle as in the landscape the river is to the mountain.

For our early human ancestors, a stable prospect for seeing-as would have been offered by the stars in the night sky. With the human eye and visual processing system relatively unchanged for hundreds of thousands of years, the stars would have been perceived as they are by modern humans, although with much clearer visibility for our early human ancestors who would not have had to contend with light pollution. For them a certain grouping of stars may have also been seen as outlining the shape of a bull or a hunter, and by convention come to be so identified. This ancient process has given rise to variable conventions in different human cultures on the identification of the constellations.

This process of symbolic seeing-as may orient pragmatic action and thus serve human survival. A journey can be guided by location of the stars, their recognition facilitated by figures seen in the sky. Knowledge of the respective locations of the stars across the seasons can be handed down from generation to generation. Beyond immediate practical purpose, such seeing-as may enable imaginative contemplation. From figures recognized in the night sky may have arisen myths among early humans about the cycles of life and death or the larger forces of the cosmos.

Recent comparative studies of prehistoric art—including the Lion-Man of the Hohlenstein-Stadel mentioned above and cave paintings from France, Spain, and Turkey—have suggested that as early as 40,000 years ago our early human ancestors had knowledge of the movements of the stars, and could track time accordingly. Comparisons of patterns found in prehistoric artworks of different places with computer-generated maps of the skies in ancient times suggest that their creators were mapping star clusters and other celestial observations. Some of the animals in these works may have also functioned as zodiac symbols.

Near the Lascaux cave entrance, for example, a painting of bulls or aurochs includes patterns of dots thought to map two different star clusters within the constellation that is known to us as Taurus. Above the shoulder of one bull appears a curved line of dots that corresponds to a map of the star cluster Pleiades. Inside the same bull figure are dots that may correspond to the Hyades cluster. In front of its snout the dots appear to represent the stars aligned in the 'belt' of the constellation Orion, which would have been visible in the sky near the Taurus constellation (Figure 2). Such symbolic connection between representations of animals on earth and the patterns of stars may have yielded a sense of connection between earth-bound humans and the larger cosmos.



We can surmise that seeing-as allowed early humans to find meaning in the world around them and in the skies above. That animals or other figures can be seen in the protrusion on a cave

**2. Cave painting in Lascaux, France, 10,000–18,000 years old, with star clusters Taurus, the Pleiades, and Orion's Belt.**

wall or in a particular grouping of stars manifests an ancient imaginative capacity amplifying human perception and gradually transforming our grasp of the surrounding world. Artistic or other representation of such subjects enables further contemplation of them. A bull or a bear seen up close may be frightening, yet the same object can become an object of reflection, and perhaps narrative, through artistic representation. Knowledge about these objects can be handed down. Beyond aiding early human survival, imagination supported the gradual emergence of human culture.

## The role of play in human cognitive development

While recent research suggests that early humans were far more sophisticated in their thinking than previously understood, early human cognition has often been compared to the childhood of the modern human mind. The role of imagination in the cognitive development of modern children has been regarded as a source of potential insight into the role imagination may have played in the cognitive evolution of the human species. We can first consider how play might have been used by prehistoric children in fostering the development of imagination.



If you take a walk today in any park, you may see young children playing with sticks, leaves, stones, or other simple objects found in the surrounding environment. While contemporary commercial societies generate countless products designed for their size and developmental age, young children enjoy playing with these basic things, often transforming them into tools, weapons, animals, or treasures. Early human children would have done the same and, like their modern counterparts, would have also adapted adult tools and utensils for their own play. Yet archaeologists have also unearthed prehistoric toys, objects constructed with no evident practical function and scaled to fit a child's hand. These give some insight into the potential role of imagination in cognitive development.

The oldest putative toys (from between 11,000 and 18,000 years ago and found in Europe) are rondelles, or small circular discs carved from stone, bone, or ivory. They are often perforated and engraved on one or both sides with animal or geometric figures. These objects were mysterious for a long period, but more recently archaeologists have begun to understand them as optical amusements. A single rondelle perforated in the centre can be used as a thaumatrope—making a kind of moving image—by being pulled on a string on its lateral axis, so that the image from one side is superimposed onto that of the other due to the persistence of images on the retina. For example, a 15,000-year-old rondelle found in 1868 in the Dordogne in France, engraved with a chamois, shows the animal on each side respectively standing and in a lying position. The disc twirled quickly would have blended and virtually animated the images for the viewer. Similar to the modern thaumatrope toy invented in the 19th century by the astronomer John Hershel and later commercialized by John Ayrton Paris, the rondelle has been likened to a prehistoric form of animation.



While adults and children may have equally delighted in such optical effects, some ancient objects appear to be solely designed for the play of young children. We can point to a 7,500-year-old stone carriage just a few inches long found in Turkey, a tiny chalk figurine of a piglet or hedgehog with a snout and long ears buried with a child from the Bronze Age at Stonehenge, and miniature figurines and rattles found in the graves of infant children in the remote Khakassia region of Siberia, including a 4,500-year-old doll carved of soapstone. On the Italian island of Pantelleria, archaeologists found part of a 4,000-year-old doll buried along with miniature cooking tools. A 3,500-year-old bronze and silver toy found in the Rhodope Mountains of Bulgaria was shaped as a stork mounted on a tripod, and could move its head, allowing children to pretend that the bird was drinking.

These miniaturizations are evidence of both advanced technical skills and social support for children's imaginative play. Just as modern dolls, stuffed animals, miniature vehicles, and building blocks do for children today, these miniaturized toys invite children to engage with and even master things in the world around them. While psychologists once argued that pretend play and imagining discouraged rational thinking in children, in recent decades the importance of play for cognitive development has begun to be recognized. In *Playing and Reality* (1971), the psychologist D. W. Winnicott argued that play nurtures a child's sense of being—'it belongs to being alive', he writes—and thus their development of a fully inhabited self. Through play children are both intensely focused and spontaneous, keenly aware of the world and their interaction with it and, through that interaction, of themselves.

More recently play has been seen as essential to the intellectual development of the child's mind. As the psychologist Paul Harris argued in *The Work of Imagination* (2000), imagining does not detract from, but is rather essential to, the development of rational thinking. Playful imagining helps children to apply knowledge they have learned from reality to new scenarios. Through imagined play children examine possible future actions, considering multiple options. By pretending they also imagine the perspectives of others, which enables social bonding and empathy. Play exercises imagination by encouraging pretence, consideration of counterfactual scenarios, and shifting perspectives. Play not only supports other skills necessary for survival, but may be an evolutionary end in itself.

While the impulse for play diminishes as children grow into adults, grown-ups also delight in pastimes with no obvious practical function, and, as Winnicott argued, play remains essential for cognitive well-being. Games that require multiple players, such as board games, were enjoyed in many ancient societies. Chequers is among the oldest board games still played and originated in Mesopotamia around 5,000 years ago. Backgammon was played in Ancient Persia (Iran), while Ancient

Egyptians played Mehen, named for the snake-god on whose shape the board is fashioned. The game of Go or Weiqi, still popular today, originated in ancient China between 3,000 and 4,000 years ago. The oldest playable board game still physically extant is an iteration of The Royal Game of Ur, originating in Mesopotamia 4,600 years ago. Its rules were written on cuneiform tablet in 177 BCE by a Babylonian astronomer. While all of these games entail complex reasoning, they also sustain the instinct for play, enabling the working out of possibilities and multiple perspectives, along with pleasurable activity.

## Animal imagination

Further evidence of the evolutionary development of imagination can be found in studies of our animal relatives. In courting rituals, male bower birds construct and elaborately decorate woven or glued towers of sticks with such objects as flowers, moss, insects, snail shells, and butterfly wings. Parrots engage in complex mimicry. Such activities may be attributed to instinct, but others are socially shared or learned. Elephants have exceptionally strong social bonds and recognize the bones of other elephants, performing burial actions suggesting awareness of death and attachment to other elephant life. Apes and monkeys use forms of language, make and use rudimentary tools, and are self-aware. While an especially concentrated ability for imagining appears to distinguish the human species, other animals can also imagine, as manifest in their problem-solving and social communication.

While throughout most of the Western tradition, animal intelligence was dismissed or denied by philosophers, Aristotle had suggested that animals must have some imagination in seeking or avoiding objects not immediately perceived. Animals have, he thought, inner visual or other percept-like representation of objects. Recent research shows that animals may be able to engage in other modes of imagining such as pretence and some creativity. Chimpanzees in the wild have been observed to transfer activities from a real scenario to a pretended object. They have been observed, for example, grooming leaves in imitation of social grooming, using sticks to fish in an 'imaginary' nest of ants, and carrying a log as if it were a baby. Even when alone they may pretend aggressive displays. Macaques may imitate one another's actions, and feign feeding or ignoring. They also play-fight and tease.

Human-raised primates exhibit a wide range of behaviours that suggest some modes of imagination. A chimp in captivity named Viki was observed to play with pretend objects, acting as if pulling at a non-existent pull toy that then got 'stuck'. A bonobo named Kanzi was observed playing with imaginary invisible objects and encouraging others to play with them. Washoe, a chimpanzee raised by humans, was the first non-human to communicate in American Sign Language. She pretended while at play, bathing her dolls with soap and drying them with towels. She and others in her group would sign 'tickle' when playing with a doll. A chimpanzee has been observed pretending to eat an eraser, signing 'eat', and subsequently hiding it in his room. This suggests imagining another perspective from which the location of a real object could be masked. In captivity gorillas have painted pictures, albeit rather rudimentary ones, to which they give titles in sign language.



Perhaps the most advanced display of animal imagination we know was evidenced by Koko, a gorilla who lived from 1971 to 2018 in California and was taught sign language from infancy. Koko came to be able to sign around 1,000 words and could understand twice as many. At play Koko routinely pretended. She played with toy gorillas, signing to them to chase or tickle each other. At around 4 years of age her favourite game was to act as if she were blind, stumbling around and bumping into things. In discussion with her caretaker about a picture of a bird, she signed

'Koko, Bird', and then admitted upon further questioning that she was in fact 'Gorilla Koko'. Upon seeing an image of the Queen of England in scarlet robes as painted by Richard Stone, Koko dressed herself up in a red blanket and signed 'Koko, Queen'. Imagination may also be at work in understanding significant events she could not perceive directly. When informed that her beloved pet kitten she had named All Ball had been struck by a car and died, Koko grieved, signing 'Bad, sad…cry-frown', and later in private audibly mourned, evidencing conscious preoccupation with something absent.

So far as we can tell, what appears to be unique to humans is the use of imagination unprompted by surrounding objects or circumstances. Only humans appear to engage in elaborated imagining apart from environmental cues, which allows us to fantasize, create fictions, and to construct other worlds. Yet evidence for higher mental functioning of apes and other animals continues to grow, and they are clearly far more advanced than we have previously believed. We now recognize that other animals besides humans—including not only primates but elephants and dolphins among others—are self-aware and may have something like an inner life. Koko's remarkable message in sign language delivered in a video to the UN Climate Change Conference in Paris in 2015 includes her criticism of 'stupid' humans who have broken nature. While staged and edited by her human companions, and so received with some scepticism about the degree of understanding involved, Koko's plea to 'Fix earth…protect earth…nature' at the very least evidenced a non-human animal evoking a situation not immediately perceived, and pointing to an alternative.

Like human cognition, non-human animal cognition arises in interaction with the environment and in efforts to shape the world to needs. Although he had dedicated his work to a phenomenology of embodied human consciousness, the French philosopher

Merleau-Ponty recognized the interiority of animal life. He noted that 'all living things, ourselves included, endeavour to give shape to a world that has not been preordained to accommodate our attempts to think and act upon it'. Yet we can hope to understand this common endeavour only 'if we are prepared to live alongside the world of animals instead of rashly denying it any kind of interiority'. To understand human imagination in light of our cognitive evolution may entail recognizing some affinities with non-human animals, however special human imagining has evolved to be.

The evolution of imagination, as we have explored in this chapter, has made human culture possible. From a modern point of view, prehistoric cave paintings, sculptures, and toys appear to express the raw vitality of early human imagination. Where our early human ancestors climbed hills and first saw the world from above, or viewed the stars with awe, modern humanity's capacities for imagining have been radically transformed by technology. We now have images of the earth from space, and can examine the whole surface of the earth by means of satellite imagery. Yet modern artists turned to so-called primitive works of early humans for inspiration. Having just seen the cave paintings at Lascaux, Picasso reportedly said, 'They invented everything.' However polemical such a statement may have been, modern artists recognized in early human art original expressions of imaginative vision.

Beyond mere survival, imagination has allowed us to amplify, transform, and expressively reflect on our experiences of living. Imagination has enabled a symbolic humanization of our world, scaled to a mental frame with which the human mind can cope and with which it can play. Due to imagination we are able to perceive the world as one to which a human community belongs. The ecological imbalance to which our practical humanization of the world has led, however, may again demand imagination as a crucial ingredient in problem-solving. In order to optimize our thinking, it may be advantageous to better understand this remarkable facility.

In the next three chapters, we will trace the philosophical understanding of imagination from the ancient Greeks to early modern philosophy and science, the rise of aesthetics and Romantic enthusiasm for imagination, and 20th-century affirmations of productive imagining.

# Chapter 3
# From divine madness to cognitive power

Throughout the history of Western thought, the concept of imagination has had a tumultuous record. Both ancient and early modern philosophers disagreed strongly about imagination, or viewed the topic with striking ambivalence. For some thinkers, imagination was at best a divinely inspired madness, at worst a source of deceptive illusion; curtailing its influence was urgent if objective truth was to be established. For others, imagination was an irrepressible activity of the mind that cannot be expelled from cognition, and may be essential to it.

Throughout their assessments, philosophers and writers considered the imagination's involvement in human thinking to be a matter of high consequence. Despite much suspicion surrounding imagination, it was intermittently understood as serving important, even essential functions for the human mind. Tracing the assessment of imagination allows us to consider a number of things: its relationship with rationality and knowledge; its role in making the images of poetry and art; and its tie to emotions, bodily sensations, empathy, and perception. These debates reveal the power of imagination and its profound implications for the imagining subject.

## The critique of imagery and appearances

In ancient Greece, where Western philosophy began, poetic literature served as a primary resource for ideas about matters both divine and human, and it is on the subject of its influence that the debate about imagination begins. The theogony of Hesiod and the epic tales of Homer had provided ancient Greek citizens with insights about the origins of the cosmos and the relevance of gods to human affairs. Dramatists such as Euripides and Sophocles provided not only entertainment but important explorations of ideas. Orators influenced public life much as political and social commentators do today.

Philosophy arose in direct contest with such literary activities. Plato's treatment of imagination must be understood in light of his effort to ensure philosophy's ascension over the influence of poetic literature and the persuasions of rhetoric. Plato aimed for victory in what he called philosophy's 'ancient quarrel' with poetry. For, in Plato's view, poets and orators had no real knowledge, and their influence was therefore dangerous.

Despite the extraordinary literary talent evidenced in his philosophical dialogues, Plato's critique of poets and artists (and implicitly of imagination) is extensive. In his dialogue *Republic*, Plato has his character Socrates advocate the censorship and even banishment of the poets on grounds that poets foster illusions and even lies. Through his protagonist, Plato lambasts poetic and artistic imagery as obscuring our apprehension of reality. He rejects poetic depictions of events, for example of a god changing form, as false and illusory. He castigates pretence—such as in drama when one actor would voice multiple characters—as detrimental to social order, for each citizen should be assigned a clear role. The polis, Plato suggests, should be governed by one whose soul is directed by reason alone, rather than a poetic—and dangerously misleading—vision of mere appearances.

In his works Plato conceptualizes imagination in several related ways: in respect to the artistic creation of images; as related to perception; and as involved with emotions. Imagination is implicated in Plato's critique of mimesis, or the production of images by poets and artists. Since he thinks of it as dealing with appearances, Plato addresses imagination in his account of their perception. He also acknowledges directly the image-making faculty of the soul, and imagination's reach into human emotions. To show how imagination was understood by Plato, we can take up each of these in turn.

Mimesis is the artistic skill of creating likenesses or, more critically, imitations, through visual or verbal images. Depictions of the bison, horses, and deer on the Chauvet cave walls described in the previous chapter are mimetic, as are Homer's depiction of the wandering of Odysseus, or the dramatic presentation of Oedipus in Sophocles' tragedy. Music can be imitative by conveying mood or feeling. The origin of all art is attributed by the ancient Greek philosophers to mimesis. Yet Plato insists that the likenesses or imitations poets and artists make are inherently misleading. Distortion by mimesis is inevitable, Plato argues, since the representation of things in poetic or visual images is several degrees removed from the true reality.



In Plato's philosophy, true being is found not in the material world that appears to perception, but rather in the stable ideas or forms accessible only to the rational part of the soul. The artist is therefore several degrees removed from such truth. In *Republic*, Socrates explains that while the craftsman makes a copy of the form of a thing—making a couch or bed, for example, according to the essential idea of a bed—the painter or poet makes only an image of that physical copy. The poet or painter's image of a bed, unlike that of the craftsman, involves no reference to an original, but only to its manifestation as appearance. Therefore, art affords not 'an imitation of things as they are', or of true reality, but only 'as they appear—of appearance [*phantasmatos*]'. This has epistemic implications, for Socrates argues that 'the creator of the phantom, the imitator, we say, knows nothing of the reality but only the appearance'.

Plato's critique of mimesis cast a long shadow in the history of art, and still figures in artists' understanding of their task. The famous example of mimesis offered in *Republic*—the bed as painted by the artist rather than made by the craftsman—has been the subject of playful critique in contemporary art. For what he called his 'combine' painting, *Bed* (1955), Robert Rauschenberg attached his own bed quilt and pillow to a frame, making a painting that was in part the real thing it represented (Figure 3). Rauschenberg was not the first modern artist to toy with mimesis, of course. Marcel Duchamp had offered his infamous submission to the Society of Independent Artists show in 1917, a 'ready-made' composed of a porcelain urinal, only signed with a fictional name by the artist. Following Duchamp, with *Bed* and other combine works, Rauschenberg advanced Pop Art, integrating into art the objects and images of everyday life that were the very things they represent.

More recently, Tracey Emin's installation *My Bed* (1998) dispensed with mimetic representation of this object altogether. Instead the artist arranged, in a dishevelled state, a box frame, mattress, used linens, pillows, and various detritus of the physical life of the artist in bed. The fact that Emin's work was nominated for the Turner Prize and, in 2014, sold at auction for several million dollars reflects not only the anti-Platonic disposition of contemporary art collectors, but ongoing play with mimesis as the supposed principle of art and challenge to its status as the paradigmatic act of imagination.

The critique of mimesis or the creation of images of things is intertwined with Plato's view of perceived images and appearances. Plato discusses *phantasia*, meaning appearances as well as their reception by the soul, and *phantasm*, designating variously appearance, apparition, dream, vision, phantom,

**3. Robert Rauschenberg, *Bed* (1955), Museum of Modern Art, New York.**

shadow, and the like. *Phantasmata* are sometimes associated with natural phenomena such as physical reflections, and sometimes with poetic or artistic imagery that in words or colours and lines creates as it were reflections of things. Among the parts of the soul identified by Plato is an image-making faculty, *eikasia*, related to the word *eikonos* (image).

Plato's use of these sets of terms bears the marks of his metaphysics, or theory of the principles underlying reality, and his epistemology, or theory of knowledge. For Plato, we recall, true being cannot be grasped in sense-experience, but only in the mind with the use of reason. What we can grasp with the senses, the empirical manifestation of reality, is mere appearance. Plato repeatedly points out that appearances can be deceptive, because a thing's appearance does not necessarily evidence its true nature. In *Republic* Socrates cites the examples of a reed that looks bent in water when in reality it is straight, and of the sun seeming small in the sky.

Plato contrasts faculties of the soul that perceive appearances and those that, in contrast, attain knowledge of a deeper reality. Plato invokes the metaphor of a divided line in order to explain the soul's cognitive distribution. The line is divided between an upper half, with its faculties of reason and understanding that pertain to knowledge, and a lower half, its faculties dealing with mere opinion. On this lower half are belief and imagination (*eikasia*). While belief deals with objects of perception (i.e. taking things as they appear), imagination deals with only images, shadows, or 'phantasms' of those objects—such as they might be depicted in literary or artistic works, or called up in the mind's eye. In the discussion of poetry, Socrates refers to the part of our thought with which images consort—represented on the lower half of the line—as inferior to 'the part that puts its trust in measurement and reckoning'—the upper part of the line. Imagination, in other words, is inferior to reason.

Imagination may also be dangerous: Plato also locates the emotions in the lower part of the soul, which is most affected by such images and without the restraint of reason. In *Republic* Plato has in mind, among other things, painful experiences such as those represented in tragic poetry. Plato is scornful of depictions of expressive lamentation and grief—since it might suggest a negative view of death or the afterlife and discourage the bravery needed to sacrifice one's life for the polis. Plato's critique of imagination encompasses its entanglement with lower emotions that, in his view, corrupt the soul and distract from contemplation of the highest objects of thought.

This rather devastating critique is, however, not the whole story about imagination for Plato. The later dialogue *Phaedrus* allows for a very different discussion of *phantasia*, of images, and of poetry. The dialogue concerns among other things the nature of eros or romantic love. The appearance of the beautiful beloved is said to awaken a higher vision of divine beauty, as it is held to be a reflection or image of its divine form or essence. In this same dialogue, Plato has Socrates admit that poets may have a gift for discerning the nature of the beautiful and, indeed, that poetry may be inspired by the gods. To be so inspired is not a form of knowledge, however. Instead Socrates calls it a form of madness, albeit one divinely endowed.

While in *Republic* Plato discusses the passive perception of appearances or the mimetic creation of images by artists and poets, in his dialogue *Philebus* he describes the active construction of images within the soul itself. There Socrates likens the soul to a book, in which memories are recorded by an inner scribe. Socrates introduces a second 'workman', namely 'a painter, who paints in our souls pictures to illustrate the words which the writer has written'. This is not merely a mnemonic function, however, for Socrates and his interlocutor agree that such writing and images in the soul relate not only experiences of the past, but also of expectations. This inner picturing is relevant to 'all hopes relating to the future'. Thus Plato recognizes imagination's role in anticipatory thought.

Despite Plato's concessions to divine inspiration and anticipation, his overall account of the imagination is admonitory. The imagination deals with epistemically suspect images and can mislead the soul from its search for knowledge and truth.

The irony of Plato's critique, of course, is that his own writings are extraordinarily imaginative. Plato uses vivid metaphors, creative analogies, imagistic illustrations, and mythical narratives. His cave parable in *Republic*, where bound individuals are watching a shadow-play on the wall as an analogy for the deceptions of sense-experience, is just one of many examples of Plato's own use of imaginative devices typically associated with poetry. Clearly Plato would have to accept imagination as a useful tool for the philosopher, so long as it is constrained by rational thought.

## Thinking images and the art of possibilities

Imagination may be more crucial to thinking than Plato recognized. Aristotle counters Plato's critique by describing imagination as an active faculty of the mind that produces images necessary for cognition. In *De Anima* (*On the Soul*), Aristotle describes that process 'by which we say that an image is presented to us', and treats *phantasia* as this image-making faculty. While Plato's account does not always distinguish between the perception of appearances and their production in the mind, Aristotle clearly distinguishes between imagination in the mind and passive sensation. He points out that through imagination visions appear to those 'even with their eyes shut'.

Aristotle notes further distinctions between imagining and sense-perception. He argues that imagination lies within our power, whereas sensation does not. Aristotle gives the example that 'we can call up a picture, as in the practice of mnemonics by the use of mental images'. He explains the visual association of the term: 'As sight is the most highly developed sense, the name *phantasia* (imagination) has been formed from *phaos* (light), because without light it is impossible to see.'

In Aristotle's view imagination need not be considered erroneous despite the fact that an image can lack grounding in reality or sharply diverge from it. In contrast to Plato, Aristotle argues that we can imagine something false without necessarily falling into error by so doing. For just as imagination is distinct from sensation, it is also distinct from belief. We can imagine the sun as a small orb in the sky, while knowing it to be many times larger than the earth. We can imagine something that in reality is not there at all, like a griffin, without believing in the image so presented. This independence of imagination from belief allows it to serve as a distinct cognitive power that can, in line with correct belief, avoid error.

The thinking soul can also be served by images as if they were contents of perception. These images can be the objects of the soul's valuation and intentions, such that the soul asserts and pursues what it deems good or denies and avoids what it deems bad. Indeed, Aristotle regards imagination as essential for any thinking at all, claiming that 'the soul never thinks without a mental image'. Aristotle specifies how thinking proceeds through such use of images. In *De Anima*, he writes:

> So the faculty of thinking then thinks the forms in images... sometimes by means of the images or thoughts in the soul, just as if it were seeing, it calculates and plans for the future in view of the present....

Here Aristotle suggests that imagination not only presents to the mind images based on past experiences, but allows us to project future possibilities. Like Socrates in Plato's *Philebus*, Aristotle acknowledges the role of anticipatory images. Closely related to this, the ability to deal in possibilities—what might or could happen, as in hypothetical thinking—is essential to innovation.

Aristotle not only recognized the ubiquity of imagination in thinking, but also valued its expression in creative works. In his *Poetics* Aristotle outlines the proper structure and elements of a successful tragedy, including the 'thought' that shapes the work as a whole. Aristotle argues that such poetry is more philosophical than history, because it tells us not only what has happened but what *could* happen. Against Plato's critique of poetic imagination, Aristotle further defends poetry and the catharsis it can provoke as beneficial for the individual soul as well as a community. While Plato warned about the dangers of provoking emotions, Aristotle thought that exercising the emotions through imaginatively stirred empathy with tragic characters has a salutary function in balancing the soul.

These connections between imagination and possibility, both in deliberative thinking and in poetic representation, suggest that imagination need not be conceived only in reproductive terms (where the imagination is only derivative of sense-experience). For if imagination is that element of our minds that allows us to think about possibilities that depart from what is already actual, imagining—or thinking that imagines—would also be the source of new ideas. Against a wholly reproductive view of imagination, philosophies of the 18th century onward promote the productive imagination. They owe much to Aristotle's recognition that imagination enables us to think possibilities.



## Embodied feeling, empathy, and trickery

Imagination evokes bodily experiences, and it was this aspect of imagination that most preoccupied some early modern thinkers. In his essay 'On the Force of Imagination' (1574), the French philosopher and essayist Michel de Montaigne offered a theory of embodied imagination that helps to explain a number of imaginative phenomena, including empathy, paranoia, and psychosomatic experiences. Montaigne argued that imagination is responsible for our ability to feel empathy for others. In his view, imagination facilitates direct communication of emotions, responses, or anxieties between one imagining subject and another. The imagination, moreover, has a direct effect on the bodily experience of the imaginer. He writes that: 'we start, tremble, turn pale, and blush, as we are variously moved by imagination'.

Most of us have had the experience of yawning after another person does so in our presence, in a kind of empathetic contagion. Montaigne explains such phenomena by reporting on his own highly sensitive empathetic responses, often through a bodily sense. He writes: 'The very sight of another's pain materially pains me. I often usurp the sensations of another person.' Through this imaginative transference, in Montaigne's example, a subject's own throat can itch when another person coughs. Before Descartes came to cast doubt on the existence of other minds, Montaigne argues that imagination gives one a quasi-direct connection with the physical or psychological experiences of another by receptively echoing or mimicking them. If another person coughs, I may cough too. If another has anxiety, this may induce anxiety in me. A cough or an anxiety is no less real even if it was provoked by imagination.

While Montaigne attested to his own experience, regarding himself afflicted or gifted with a strong imagination, contemporary psychology has studied the phenomenon of social empathy. Some cognitive theories describe this ability as the mind's simulation of the experience of another. Neuroscientists have identified a mirror neuron mechanism in the brain in which neurons are triggered when observing another perform a given action. Such explanations point, respectively, to the cognitive processes and brain mechanics underlying empathetic experiences as described by Montaigne. While these accounts help to explain the cognitive and physical correlates of social empathy, imagination remains their experiential medium.

Empathy is not limited to an immediate, unconscious response, but can be cultivated by deliberate effort to imagine the perspective of another. Literature has been credited with fostering empathetic imagining. Aristotle counted pity or empathy for the suffering of characters among the core emotions stirred up by tragic drama. In *Poetic Justice* (1995), philosopher Martha Nussbaum promoted the view that literature helps us to imagine, and thus empathize with, perspectives of others unlike ourselves, and that the literary imagination thus serves a democratic function. More recently theorists have argued that literature functions to exercise our 'theory of mind'—the idea that we recognize others as having experiences like our own, that we can 'mind-read'. This may be multiply layered in literary experience—as when we can imagine the points of view of multiple characters and their perspectives on one another—but also forms a part of our basic human communication. Enabled by imagination, we recognize others as having experiences as we ourselves do, though these experiences are not directly accessible to us.

Apart from embodied empathy, Montaigne offers a number of engaging examples that demonstrate the imagination not only as a feature of mental life but as a bodily force. He cites the variable effects of imagination on erotic activity, and what we now call the placebo effect, in which substances we believe to have healing or other beneficial powers induce such effects based on our beliefs. He wonders if religious devotion might have similar effects on our well-being, thus anticipating some contemporary studies in empirical psychology. (While there is no scientific evidence (at time of writing) that prayer directly affects health, visualization techniques have been demonstrated to positively affect subjects' well-being.)

Montaigne's speculations, however, go beyond the scope of plausibility. In the absence of scientific scrutiny, he wonders whether one could bring about physical effects in the world through the imagination alone. He notes, for example, an anecdote about a falconer said to bring down a kite with his gaze. Such speculations would have inflamed anxiety about imagination in Montaigne's time.

Philosophers were not the only thinkers invested in understanding imagination. In a number of his dramatic works, Shakespeare explored the power of imagination, but expressed more scepticism than Montaigne did about its efficacy. In *A Midsummer Night's Dream* (1605), a comedy featuring fairies and spells and magical metamorphoses, imagination is humorously attacked as a source of error, and as stimulating hysteria and obsession. Shakespeare's treatment of imagination in the play is also analytical. Observing the misadventures of others, Theseus comments on the distortions wrought by imagination, and implicates the audience as among those duped by its charms.

For just as the characters succumb to trances and hallucinations, the audience is drawn into the world of the play and subjected to its extraordinary fantasies. Commenting on the visions 'more strange than true' of imagination, Theseus says:

> The poet's eye, in fine frenzy rolling,
> Doth glance from heaven to Earth, from Earth to heaven.
> And as imagination bodies forth
> The forms of things unknown, the poet's pen
> Turns them to shapes and gives to airy nothing
> A local habitation and a name.

The poet, Theseus suggests, is as irrational as the lover and the lunatic. While the mad person would see demons everywhere, he tells us, the lover is duped by fantasies of his beloved's superior beauty. Shakespeare comes close to suggesting that the capacity to be misled by imagination is a universal human vulnerability. The author of *A Midsummer Night's Dream* seems to take extended delight in elaborating the dubious exercises of the poet's fancy in particular.

Here Shakespeare ironically echoes Plato's critique of poets in *Republic*. The poet is not merely misled by imagination, but, in and through imagining, deliberately misleads others—his audience and readers. While the lover and the lunatic are helpless under imagination's sway, the poet's imagination is intentional and directed. Shakespeare charges that imagination tends to fabricate causation in place of mere coincidence and, in provoking fear, transforms neutral objects into dangers. Shakespeare here anticipates the notion of productive imagination, insofar as he further charges that imagination prompts false inferences—apprehending some joy, the imagination furnishes an idea of an agent who brought it forth. Seeing a bush on a dark evening, we might fear it as a bear. Imagination conjures from nothing and transforms what is present in ways that provoke our emotions, entrap our thoughts, and potentially misdirect our deeds. Imagination breeds superstition and paranoia—along with comedic amusements.

We cannot find physical sustenance or shelter in fantasies, and Shakespeare accordingly points to imagination's poverty. In *Richard II*, Shakespeare has Bolingbroke remind us that imagination is not equal to reality, by invoking contrasting sensations:



> Oh! who can hold a fire in his hand
> By thinking on the frosty Caucasus?
> Or cloy the hungry edge of appetite
> By bare imagination of a feast?

We could hold a fire in our hands but we cannot prevent our hands from being burned by thinking of frosty mountains. We cannot sate our appetite with mere thoughts. The irony would not have been lost on Shakespeare that he uses vivid imagery to expose imagination's limits.

## Methodical imagination and the synthesis of experience

If imagination provoked anxiety among those of the early modern period, some set out to curtail imagination's power. Descartes sought to differentiate the rational part of the mind from that of imagination. While imagination was recognized as mediating between the senses and the intellect—bringing ideas of corporeal things to mind—it must not, in Descartes's view, have undue influence. At stake was not only a contest between philosophy and the imaginative arts, but trust in the mind's grasp of rational ideas that were to serve as the foundations of modern science.

For Descartes, rational thinking and imagination both deal with ideas in the mind, yet they are distinct faculties and the former alone will be considered essential to cognition. To confuse the source of our ideas not only risks error. It also renders unstable any effort to grasp the nature of reality through rational ideas.

Thus, in the *Meditations on First Philosophy* (1641), Descartes aligns the imagination with perceptual distortions, illusions, and madness. According to Descartes, innate ideas are clear and distinct, but ideas borne of imagination are merely derivative, copied from sense-impressions and recombined, and may be experienced as delusions or hallucinations. Descartes describes persons who have succumbed to the imagination so that:

> they steadfastly insist that they are kings when they are utter paupers, or that they are arrayed in purple robes when they are naked, or that they have heads made of clay, or that they are gourds, or that they are made of glass.

Descartes further argues that thinking can proceed without imagination, and so imagination is not an essential part of the thinking self.

While Descartes's own philosophical procedures will employ imagination in distinctive and fascinating ways, here and in his work *Discourse on Method* (1637) the imagination is treated dismissively as associated with the uncertain and epistemically problematic life of the senses. In the *Discourse* Descartes anticipates his arguments in the *Meditations* and argues for the priority of reason, as the faculty capable of clear and distinct ideas, over imagination and the sense-experience from which it draws. Descartes argues that epistemic vigilance—the use of reasoned judgement to curtail the influence of images—is needed to counter imagination, for 'it is not a dictate of Reason that what we thus see or imagine is in reality existent'.

Despite declaring imagination to be inessential to the rational mind, Descartes allows some role for imagining in both his philosophical and his scientific writings. In fact, Descartes engages imagination methodically in *Meditations*. Just as Plato engages imagery, metaphor, and myth, Descartes engages pretence, hypothetical constructions, and visualization as tools for his methodical process of doubt. The thought experiments in the *Meditations* would not be achievable without imagination as both the medium of such counterfactual images and their very theme.

The *Meditations* begins with Descartes purporting to excise from his mind all accumulated opinions, including those drawn from sense-experience, in order to establish a truthful basis for scientific thinking. The thinker's own existence as a thinking being is the one indubitable truth that can serve as a point of reference, a basis for rational thinking as such. But arriving at this basic truth requires a methodical use of the imagination. Descartes must contrast his certain grasp of himself as a thinking mind with counterfactual possibilities—most famously with the prospect that an evil deceiver makes him think that he exists—in order to exclude them as logically incoherent. Descartes argues that he may be deceived about his body, but he cannot be deceived that he is, at very least, a 'thinking thing'. For one who doubts his own existence must exist in order to doubt it in the first place.

Imagination is also necessary to contemplate what knowledge we may have of the world. In the *Discourse* Descartes defines imagination as the ability to contemplate 'the shape of a corporeal thing'. Imagination allows the mind both to conjure ideas of things that could belong to the world of the senses and to contemplate or manipulate such ideas. Imagination is required for the mind to construct a representation of the world to which its scientific understanding could apply.

We can find an example of this in Descartes's own scientific studies. In explaining how a rainbow appears in the sky, Descartes imagines a point of view from which light, hitting the raindrops at a particular angle, would produce colour. Without this hypothetical visualization Descartes could not have explained the phenomenon. While he insists that imagination is not an essential part of the thinking subject, Descartes concedes in the *Discourse* that even ideas originating in imagination must 'contain in them some truth'.

A development in consideration of imagination occurs a century later, when the Scottish philosopher David Hume will assign further roles to imagination—that of not only providing ideas of corporeality but also synthesizing them. In *An Enquiry Concerning Human Understanding* (1748), Hume describes the various capacities we ought to attribute to imagination. With imagination we can engage in fictional constructions, feigning (what we have called pretence) and rendering (through envisioning) such appearances convincingly. He writes:

> Nothing is more free than the imagination of man; and though it cannot exceed that original stock of ideas furnished by the internal and external senses, it has unlimited power of mixing, compounding, separating, and dividing these ideas, in all the varieties of fiction and vision.

While the imagination is at first described in Hume's account in positive terms, as free and capable, his description of what imagination does is limited to a reproductive function. Imagination does not truly create anything new, but mixes, adds together, takes apart, or divides other ideas.

The difficulty arises with the potential inextricability of imagination and belief. While Aristotle segregated these capacities, Hume does not. Of imagination, Hume continues:

> It can feign a train of events, with all the appearance of reality, ascribe to them a particular time and place, conceive them as existent, and paint them out to itself with every circumstance, that belongs to any historical fact, which it believes with the greatest certainty.

As Shakespeare pointed out, the imagination can evoke fictional worlds not only conceived as existing, but believed as such. While Aristotle had taken pains to distinguish between imagination of and belief in a false image, Hume follows Shakespeare in attributing to imagination's feigning a potential concession to the existence of its objects.



As an empiricist philosopher Hume also recognized—despite his critique of imagination—that only imagination can facilitate the connections among our ideas drawn from sense-experience, providing a crucial synthetic function for the mind. Sense-data does not of itself give us a stable presentation of the world. Imagination, for Hume, binds sense-data together to enable us to perceive the objects of perception from moment to moment as constant, enabling a coherent experience of them. Hume argued that imagination also creates the sense of personal identity, as well as of the continuity of objects in space and time, by synthesizing as it were all the diverse data of which these entities are composed. As he wrote in *A Treatise of Human Nature* (1739):

> The identity, which we ascribe to the mind of man, is only a fictitious one, and of a like kind with that which we ascribe to vegetables and animal bodies. It... must proceed from a like operation of the imagination upon like objects.

In Hume's account there would be no coherent sense of a stable objective world or of our own selves without imagination. This view, adapted and developed by Kant, will inspire extravagant expectations of imagination among philosophers over the next two centuries.

The critical scrutiny and even condemnation of imagination in ancient and early modern philosophy are countered by a recognition of its power and importance for the human mind. Imagination's role in literature and the arts has been historically opposed to the philosophical search for truth. Imagination's relation to truth and falsity, sensation and emotion has been scrutinized not only by philosophers but by literary writers considering its power. The delusions and distortions attributed to imagination provoked anxiety over its influence in human thinking.

At the same time, imagination has also been recognized as the medium of empathy and for providing the mind with an intuition of the objective world. With much ambivalence, philosophers come to recognize that imagination may be involved in shaping cognition of the world and of ourselves. Recognition of the synthetic power of imagination will play an important role in the formulation of the productive imagination. This notion will in turn electrify the aesthetics of the late 18th and 19th centuries and influence treatment of the imagination long into the 20th, as we will see in the following chapters.

# Chapter 4
# The productive and aesthetic imagination

The assessment and understanding of imagination was transformed by the recognition of its central role in the perception and expression of aesthetic qualities. From the Greek word *aisthesthai* ('perceive'), aesthetics originally meant the study of sense-perception. But by the 18th century, philosophers of aesthetics focused on the perception of beauty or sublimity—the sense of the vast or transcendent—in nature or art. Practitioners of aesthetics tried to identify the nature of aesthetic pleasure and to unlock the secrets of artistic genius. Imagination came to be appreciated as the source of our experience of freedom and even of the very feeling of life. As rationality, with the scientific revolution, had come to be associated with knowledge of a physically determined and mathematically predictable world, some philosophers looked to imagination to enliven the mind and offer glimpses of a higher meaning.

The rise of aesthetics (and particularly its treatment by Kant) would inspire an ecstatic devotion to imagination on the part of the Romantic writers and thinkers. Celebrating the productive imagination, early 19th-century Romantics found in it an echo of divine creation or an ability to intuit what they called the 'absolute' or immediate, unconditioned knowledge of reality in its wholeness. Later that century, the German philosopher Friedrich Nietzsche claimed that imagination was a vital cognitive force, and thought that through art, imagination could counter the cold, abstract thinking that constricted modern life and impeded reception of nature's primal forces. In this chapter we trace the discovery of productive imagination—imagination which does not merely reproduce sense-experience but originally generates connections or ideas—and its profound legacy.

## Shaping the phenomenal world

Productive imagination plays a number of roles in Kant's philosophy. According to Kant, the coherence of the phenomenal world—of the world as it appears to us—requires the activity of what he called the productive imagination. Taking Hume's idea that imagination synthesizes sense-perception, Kant argued further that imagination contributes to shaping how we experience the world before us. Imagination in this role works in the service of perception, bringing the manifold of sensation—the diverse data of sense-experience—into an image for the mind.

Kant advances beyond Hume's idea of the synthetic role for imagination in clearly distinguishing the productive use of imagination from any merely reproductive function. Kant defines imagination as the 'faculty of intuition without the presence of the object'. Yet Kant explains in his work *Anthropology from a Pragmatic Point of View* (1798) that imagination can work reproductively or productively. The reproductive imagination allows us to reproduce the idea or image of any objects we have already experienced. It is, as Kant writes, a 'derivative presentation'. In contrast, the productive imagination produces an 'original presentation', making possible any experience of an object in the first place.

To understand how the imagination can function productively, we need to address one of Kant's several terms for imagination. When he refers to imagination by the term *Einbildungskraft*, the German term suggests the power (*Kraft*) for making a unified or single (*ein*) image (*Bild*). *Einbildungskraft* is described by Kant as the synthetic power to make present a coherent image from the diversity of impressions we receive from our senses. Kant's term *Phantasie* (which can be translated as 'imagination' or 'fantasy' in English) can indicate the playful inner combination or transformation of such images when they are called to mind. *Vorstellungskraft*—or the power (*Kraft*) of ideation or presentation (*Vorstellung*)—is also important as the power to represent, as in conjuring an idea or intuition of something. In Kant's writings, these terms sometimes designate technical assignments of imagination, while at other times they are used interchangeably. It is as *Einbildungskraft* that imagination is conceived as productive in a way fundamental to our experience.



In his ground-breaking work *Critique of Pure Reason* (1781) Kant outlined our cognition of objects, or our perception and understanding of things in the world. He argued that several of our cognitive faculties—sensibility, understanding, and reason—work together to give coherent form to phenomenal experience, or to the world as it appears to us. How the world is in itself apart from such appearance, we cannot know. Kant likened this to a 'Copernican revolution'. Kant argued that reality appears as it does to us because it is so structured by the mind. Our sense of reality is structured for us according to our own cognitive set-up.

Imagination for Kant is part of the faculty of sensibility, which also includes the capacity for sensations—both outer senses of the spatial world and the inner sense of temporally ordered states of mind. Kant argued that imagination is responsible for synthesizing sensations which are subsumed under—or given order by—the categories of the understanding. This means that we experience the world not merely as a barrage of sensory input but rather in a spatial, temporal, and causal continuity and according to an objective order which the mind can interpret. For this to happen, Kant writes, 'imagination is to bring the manifold of intuition into the form of an image'—or the diverse impressions in the mind are put together to form a discrete whole. This unified intuition will come together with, and (as Kant puts it) be legislated by, the faculty of understanding. In this role imagination is productive because its synthetic process, underwritten automatically by the mind, yields an original presentation. Imagination does not merely re-present what we have already experienced in perception, but plays an original role in shaping the perception itself.

Productive imagination for Kant is thus 'transcendental', as it exceeds the bounds of a single faculty to provide an underlying foundation for experience. Imagination in this mode is performed spontaneously, Kant says, for it is not derivative of or directed by another faculty of mind. This notion of spontaneity will become important for Kant's understanding of aesthetic experience. For the Romantics, this spontaneity will link the imagination to human freedom. Aesthetic experience, moreover, will be celebrated for promoting the 'free play' of imagination with the understanding—a role in which imagination is not subordinate to, but plays together with, conceptual thinking.



## Aesthetic free play and the perception of beauty

Recognition of the transcendental role of productive imagination leaves us with a difficulty, one that also pertains to contemporary theories of creativity, as we will see in Chapter 6. If imagination is always operating to shape our phenomenal experience, how is a particularly 'imaginative' experience different from the ordinary processing of input from our surroundings? The philosophical discipline of aesthetics sought to distinguish particularly heightened experiences, such as the feelings evoked by beautiful nature or art, from ordinary perception. It is to Kant's aesthetic philosophy that we can look for an account of what he called the beautiful and the sublime, as well as artistic genius. In its special aesthetic roles, imagination will turn out to be of central importance for reconciling the mind and the world.

Aesthetics arose in the mid-18th century, when the German philosopher Alexander Baumgarten applied the philosophy of perception more generally to experiences of beauty in nature and art. The Irish-born philosopher Edmund Burke had also tried to grasp the ways we are affected by the experiences of the beautiful and the sublime. Both thinkers sought to explain the significance of those special experiences that seem to be universal: a feeling of pleasure taken in beautiful nature or in works of artistic genius, and of awe in encountering sublime vistas or ideas. Kant understood from these sources, among others, that his own philosophy would have been incomplete without grasping such experiences, for they stand apart strikingly from a deterministic understanding of the world. He also recognized in them the prospect of joining two otherwise separate parts of his philosophy. Kant devoted the third of his so-called critical works, the *Critique of Judgment* (1790), to how the perception of beauty and sublimity engages imagination in distinctive ways.



Kant found that aesthetic experience interrupts our usual cognitive habits. In ordinary experience, Kant had argued, the understanding 'legislates' the intuitions shaped through imagination, imposing upon them conceptual coherence and ensuring our grasp of a knowable reality. Yet when confronted with a beautiful object, the subject's ordinary thinking processes are for a moment suspended in the experience of pleasure. The judgement that something, say a sunset, 'is beautiful' pertains not to the object itself, Kant claims, but to the feeling it provokes in the experiencing subject. This feeling is initiated when, encountering something beautiful, the imagination and the understanding engage in a playful mode of interaction. Instead of the imagination being 'legislated' by the understanding, the experience of beauty stimulates a cognitive 'free play' between them, which enlivens the mind.

This mental vitality is described by Kant as a 'feeling of life': a feeling of freedom that importantly differs from our understanding of a world wholly determined by material causes. In *Critique of Pure Reason* Kant had explained knowledge of reality through the lens of Newtonian physics: the world we know is a mechanistic universe causally determined with mathematical precision. But he also regarded the human soul as free, and therefore capable of autonomous legislation of its desires, which he described in his second critical work, *Critique of Practical Reason* (practical here meaning pertaining to morality). While the phenomenal world, or the world we can know, is causally determined, the noumenal world, or the world as it is in itself, includes the free human self or soul.

These realms known by pure and practical reason respectively are absolutely separate. Kant says in the preface to *Critique of Judgment* that an abyss (the German term is *Abgrund*) yawns between them. Yet encountering beauty, we are affected by an object in the phenomenal world the effect of which cannot be wholly explained in mechanical or deterministic terms. Such experience offers a glimpse of what Kant considers our higher moral calling and, implicitly, of our freedom.

Let us consider the example of aesthetic experience mentioned above. According to Kant, perceiving a beautiful sunset stimulates imagination in a free play with understanding. Of course, in ordinary cognition, we understand the sunset in practical or scientific terms. A sailor might consider a particularly red sunset as indicating clear weather from the west in the morning. A physicist might describe the sunset as a scattering of light rays when they strike molecules in the atmosphere, at a time of day when, due to the earth's rotation, the sunlight takes a longer pathway to reach the human eye. Yet insofar as it strikes us as beautiful, the sunset is not wholly explained away by this practical or physical knowledge. Such determinations are suspended as the mind absorbs the phenomenon in a state of play. For the beautiful sunset evokes a special form of pleasure and with that an awareness of another aspect of ourselves. When I judge the sunset as beautiful, it is for me more than a practical indication or a set of physical effects. In such experience, Kant says, the 'understanding serves the imagination rather than vice versa'.

Although the judgement of the beautiful is subjective, Kant claims that it is also universal, and so connects us with our common humanity. When we experience a beautiful sunset, Kant suggests, we feel a connection to other human subjects, for we feel that they too would be similarly affected if they too were to view the sunset. Indeed, when we witness something beautiful we may feel an impulse to share it with another, pointing out to them how beautiful it is, despite the fact that there is more to it than we can put into words. And although we cannot explain it, the beauty of the sunset will evoke the purposefulness of nature as a whole—a sense that it all fits together in some way that is not merely random but expresses a higher purpose. This happens, Kant argues, without the mind's supplying any concept of what this purpose may be. This cognitive free play thus sustains within the subject an orientation towards the world as a purposive, harmonious whole.



Beauty is often explained by reference to the concept of symmetry and our attraction to it. Yet Kant argues that freedom is central to any lasting effect beauty may have upon us. For Kant a judgement of the beautiful is not a determination of the object, but an effect of imagination in the process of perceiving it. In aesthetic terms, perfect regularity eventually bores us, Kant claims, while phenomena that stimulate imagination's free play captivate us. To illustrate this, Kant praises the wildness of English gardens, as opposed to the strictly geometric French designs popular at the time. These and similar phenomena—Kant mentions a pepper garden in the forest of Sumatra, the play of birdsong, a flickering fire, or the rippling of a brook—carry 'the imagination's freedom very far'. The pleasure we take in such phenomena reveals the freedom of imagination which thrives with no requirement to conform to an idea of perfection.

Free play in experiencing the beautiful may also stimulate creative activity or the making of beautiful art. Artistic creativity, Kant says, is that power to 'create another nature out of the material that actual nature gives it'. Here Kant also introduces the notion of the aesthetic ideas—ideas borne by poetry or art that provoke intuitions to which no concept is adequate.

> By an aesthetical idea I understand that representation of the imagination which prompts much thought, but to which no determinate thought whatsoever, i.e. no [determinate] concept, can be adequate; so that no language can express it completely and allow us to grasp it.

Aesthetic ideas, Kant argues, expand our thinking, for they allow us to 'strive toward something that lies beyond the bounds of experience'. Despite its ineffability, an aesthetic idea prompts the mind to 'think more', beyond conceptual reason, thus enlivening the mind.



## Imagination and the sublime

While in perceiving or creating the beautiful, the imagination is freely playful, the sublime provokes a different response—one of violent agitation of the imagination. A major theme in Romanticism, the sublime was thought to be an important aesthetic experience. The sublime may be experienced through witnessing natural phenomena that seem overwhelming in their power or scale, or invoked by ideas of such magnitude they surpass imaginative intuition.

In his work *A Philosophical Enquiry into the Origin of our Ideas of the Sublime and Beautiful* (1757), Burke emphasized terrifying, dangerous phenomena that, when experienced from a position of safety, could provoke a negative form of pleasure or awe. Echoing Aristotle's analysis of tragic pleasure taken in depictions of catastrophic suffering, Burke wanted to explain the feeling of delight we take in objects that would elicit our strongest emotions. The sublime is an experience that evokes emotions pertaining to self-preservation, and produces astonishment:

> The passion caused by the great and sublime in nature, when those causes operate most powerfully, is Astonishment; and astonishment is that state of the soul, in which all its motions are suspended, with some degree of horror. In this case the mind is so entirely filled with its object, that it cannot entertain any other, nor by consequence reason on that object which employs it.

The sublime evokes a sense of boundlessness that surpasses anything we could create ourselves or even fully comprehend, and as the mind is overwhelmed by the sublime other 'motions of the soul' are suspended.



Sublime phenomena may include a tumultuous ocean, powerful thunderstorms, earthquakes, erupting volcanoes. These would be the kinds of objects that Kant, in *Critique of Judgment*, argued stimulate a sense of the 'dynamically sublime'. In the face of these, the mind strains to intuit the boundlessness and magnitude of the forces involved—and insofar as it does not resolve on such an intuition, lingers in astonishment. For 'nature is sublime in those of its appearances whose intuition carries with it the idea of their infinity'. To witness the sublime, at least from a safe distance, is to experience 'an expansion of the mind'. Yet the power of nature is also demystified by the sublime, insofar as the mind is able to resist the presentation of such overwhelming force.

In addition to manifestations of natural power, for Kant the sublime is triggered by phenomena the magnitude of which dwarfs human perception. The immensity of some phenomena overwhelms our power to assemble an image of their unity—Kant names the Egyptian pyramids, the Swiss Alps, and St Peter's Basilica in Rome. Having never ventured further than 10 miles from his native Prussian city of Königsberg, Kant never saw these sights in person. Yet Kant could have imagined that in order to take them in as a whole, one would have to stand so far back from them that one could no longer perceive minutiae. The imagination must strain, and fail, to encompass simultaneously the unity of such objects and the diversity of their details. While such effort does expand the imagination, Kant argues, a kind of violence is inflicted on the subject's inner sense. Yet, as Kant argues, 'this same violence that the imagination inflicts on the subject is still judged purposive for the *whole vocation* of the mind'. The awe we experience in the sublime calls forth our own higher vocation as human beings.

Natural phenomena associated with the sublime are persistent subjects of Romantic painting, despite Kant's view that art could not properly represent the sublime. Works by the German painter Caspar David Friedrich—such as *The Monk by the Sea* (1808–10)—contemplate the magnificence of natural scenes in which the human figure may be diminutive. The English painter J. M. W. Turner depicted forces of nature in episodes of great destruction, including great raging fires, devastating naval battles, or ships swallowed up at sea by enveloping storms—as in *Snow Storm—Steam-Boat off a Harbour's Mouth* (first exhibited in 1842). It was Turner's particular genius to evoke for the viewer a sense of the boundlessness of the sublime from within the spatial confines of the painted image. The tumultuous, misty, swirling, and enveloping colours of Turner's sea storm scenes not only express the Romantic sublime but will come to influence Abstract Expressionist renderings of nature.

Yet ideas might represent the sublime more than art could, according to Kant. The idea of the end of all things or of infinity could overwhelm the human imagination with its magnitude. The mind cannot invent an image or conjure a sensuous intuition that adequately corresponds to such a concept as infinity, which Kant included among examples of what he called the 'mathematically sublime'. These sorts of ideas, in their provocation of astonishment, seem at first to expose the inadequacy of the human mind, or more specifically that of imagination. Yet the resolution of astonishment turns out to involve what the French philosopher Jean-François Lyotard, in his contemporary revival of Kant in *Lessons on the Analytic of the Sublime* (1991), likened to a sacrifice of imagination to the power of reason. For Kant, the experience of the sublime ultimately, and paradoxically, reveals the human superiority over nature. For rational thought prevails over the imagination and the inadequate images it forms from the empirical world.

While frightening, the sublime also 'calls forth our strength' to regard our physical vulnerability to nature's forces as subordinate to our higher calling. According to Kant the experience of the sublime provokes us to test in our imaginations the highest value we hold of ourselves as human beings, were we in a position to have to choose, for example, between saving ourselves and upholding a higher moral law. Experiencing the sublime reminds us of our ability to consider ideas that exceed any presentation in the phenomenal world, and potentially choose even in the face of mortal danger what action we judge to be right. This for Kant demonstrates our capacity for moral autonomy, and thus our human dignity.



## From cosmic speculation to the 'absolute'

The rise of aesthetics ignited rapture about the imagination across the Romantic movement. Coleridge had read Kant for many years before publishing his famous definition of imagination in *Biographia Literaria* in 1817. For Coleridge, the imagination is central to the human self and our knowledge of the world. It offers our only access to the intuition of nature's unity and to the divine.

The definition of imagination offered by Coleridge, however, is notoriously confusing. Coleridge employed three terms for imagination, distinguishing among the primary imagination, the secondary imagination, and fancy. Fancy appears to describe the reproductive, derivative imagination, as in the ability to conjure and recombine images of things not present to immediate perception. But imagination proper is identified by Coleridge as a genuinely creative power. Kant's emphasis on productivity and spontaneity is reflected in Coleridge's description of the primary imagination and its secondary echo.

The primary imagination is ravishingly praised as a vital power allowing for finite human beings to repeat the creativity of God by perceiving creation. Coleridge writes:

> The primary imagination I hold to be the living power and prime agent of all human perception, and as a repetition in the finite of the eternal act of creation of the infinite I AM. The secondary I consider as an echo of the former, coexisting with the conscious will, yet still identical with the primary in the kind of its agency, and differing only in degree, and in the mode of its operation.



Primary imagination is a vital, original agency, and yet it is also receptive insofar as it is involved in and affects all perception. We can perceive aspects of nature as beautiful or sublime, for example, due to this 'living power' of imagination. As the 'prime agent' in perception itself, imagination allows the poet or artist to receive inspiration from divinely endowed nature. This echoes Plato's argument, in *Phaedrus*, that poets can uniquely perceive the beautiful, and are divinely inspired.

Yet for Coleridge imagination must also function in conjunction with human will. The primary imagination in human perception itself repeats in finite terms the divine generative act which gives shape to the world as it is experienced. The secondary imagination is 'an echo of' this primary creative power, but fainter, 'differing in degree', and it operates at the level of human consciousness.

With secondary imagination, an artist may intentionally create, impose, and discover ideas in the act of creating. Thus, while the secondary imagination is most relevant to the creation of beauty in art, it follows and is subordinate to the primary imagination endowing a more original perception of beauty in nature.

The ancient notion of divine inspiration is thus here joined with an account of imagination as a faculty of human cognition. While implying receptivity to a higher power (the primary imagination), the imagination (as secondary) is also rooted in the active human mind. Through imagination thought can go beyond direct perception, or the retrieval and combination of its sense impressions in fancy, and enable higher cognition. Taken together, the power of imagination enables the human mind both to perceive and understand the created universe and to create works that echo its divine arrangements.



Yet the importance of imagination goes far beyond its role in human creativity. In a letter of 16 October 1797, Coleridge credits imaginative elements of his childhood education with preparing him for understanding the vastness of the universe. He describes how his grasp of astronomy—and its sublime scale—was supported by fantastical literary tales.

> I remember, that at eight years old I walked with my father one winter evening from a farmer's house... & he told me the names of the stars—and how Jupiter was a thousand times larger than our world—and that the other twinkling stars were Suns that had worlds rolling round them... I heard him with a profound delight & admiration; but without the least mixture of wonder or incredulity. For from my early reading of Faery Tales, & Genii &c &c—my mind had been habituated *to the Vast*—& I never regarded *my senses* in any way as the criteria of my belief.

Here Coleridge credits his readiness for the cosmological expansion of his mind to literature. Even fantastical tales have their place as an antidote to strict empiricism, elevating the mind to entertain ideas beyond direct observation.

Without imagination, Coleridge suggests, our understanding would lack any cosmologically unifying principles. He argues that we would be able to 'contemplate nothing but *parts*' rather than the whole. Coleridge may have had in mind Giordano Bruno, a 16th-century monk who speculated about both the infinity of the universe and the coexistence of multiple worlds. Bruno's speculations anticipated the contemporary theory of the multiverse, positing that the observable universe is but one among many occupying other regions of space-time.

While rejecting narrowly empirical education, Coleridge also argues that strictly rationalist education would be insufficient. Strict rationality in the absence of imagination would lead to 'microscopic acuteness'. Such a mind would be unable to conceive of any cosmic order. Moreover, reason alone would not prepare the mind for the perception of beauty, of the sublime, or for any intuition of a higher meaning.

This view of the imagination as not merely reproductive but as an active power of the mind is echoed by William Wordsworth, for whom imagination endows our experience with transcendent meaning that exceeds direct perception. In *The Prelude* Wordsworth writes of imagination extending the eye beyond the path over the horizon as 'an invitation into space | Boundless, or guide into eternity'. For Wordsworth productive imagination allows us to go beyond the bounds of ordinary experience and access a higher reality.

Yet the imagination also opens the subject to disruption. For as Wordsworth's speaker suggests, nature may be glimpsed through imagination as 'a dim and undetermined sense | Of unknown modes of being'. Imagination may leave the subject feeling bereft. As he writes in the 1799 version of *The Prelude*:

...In my thoughts
There was a darkness—call it solitude,
Or blank desertion—no familiar shapes
Of hourly objects, images of trees,
Of sea or sky, no colours of green fields,
But huge and mighty forms that do not live
Like living men moved slowly through my mind
By day, and were the trouble of my dreams.

Despite the surrounding nature, with imagination the subject may be left in a state of isolation, of 'blank desertion'. While imagination affords an experience of nature as beautiful, it also induces thoughts of the uncanny.

The idea that the familiarity of nature can break down, and that our relation to it must be mediated by imagination, is proposed by the German poet Friedrich Hölderlin, an early Romantic who like Coleridge was profoundly influenced by Kant's aesthetic philosophy. In his two-stanza poem 'The Half of Life', for example, Hölderlin's speaker presents, in the first stanza, the warmth and glory of summer which seems to embrace the speaker, and in the second, lifeless winter which appears 'speechless and cold'. Similarly, the eponymous protagonist of Hölderlin's novel *Hyperion* (1797) oscillates between a feeling of belonging to nature and one of despairing loss, a cycle which finds no narrative resolution. Yet in a draft of a preface for the novel Hölderlin cited the experience of beauty as a potential restoration of our lost unity with nature. For a time in thrall to Kantian aesthetics, Hölderlin recognized the free play of imagination in the experience of beauty as the prospect of a restored vitality for the human subject.

As it did for Hölderlin, aesthetic theory electrified other German Romantics, who identified in imagination the key to achieving a grasp of the 'absolute'. While understood in different ways, the absolute may signify the infinite whole encompassing all of being or, more simply, intuitive and immediate access to nature as it is in itself. The absolute could never be known directly through rational means or fully expressed in conceptual thought. Yet Romantic thinkers held out the prospect that it may be glimpsed in poetic or aesthetical intuition, for which imagination would play a crucial role.

An important Romantic theorist, Friedrich Schlegel thought that imagination was requisite for grasping true reality. As he wrote in *Philosophical Fragments*: 'No poetry, no reality. Just as there is, despite all the senses, no external world without imagination.' Furthering Kant's idea that imagination may function in a state of free play, Schlegel argued for 'the creative philosophy that originates in freedom and belief in freedom, and shows how the human spirit impresses its law on all things and how the world is its work of art'. Like Coleridge, Schlegel argued that imagination, as 'man's faculty for perceiving divinity', was required for any religious sense.

Further Romantic elaborations of the productive imagination attribute to it new powers. For Novalis (the pen name of the German poet Georg Philipp Friedrich Freiherr von Hardenberg), the human imagination, rather than merely allowing us to escape the constraints of nature, offered access to its inner secrets. His novel *Heinrich von Ofterdingen* (1802) is a psychological reflection on the inner life of its protagonist and defends the importance of imagination and its visions. In an opening scene, Heinrich discusses with his parents a dream from which he has just awoken. Heinrich recounts seeing a blue flower which bore the face of his beloved. This recurring image of the blue flower would be widely recognized among Romantics as a symbol of longing and of the unification for which we ultimately long, becoming a symbol of Romanticism in works by E. T. A. Hoffmann, Walter Benjamin, and C. S. Lewis. While Heinrich's father dismisses Heinrich's dream, Heinrich argues that it may allow a glimpse of the inner self otherwise veiled to us. The blue flower can also be read as representing the power of the imagination itself. For the dream vision stimulates, along with intense yearning, explicit reflection on the place of imagination in human life and knowledge.

Novalis planned in his notebooks to create a Romantic encyclopaedia that would gather diverse human knowledge in a single text. Such a project would not only collect but synthesize science, philosophy, religion, poetics, and aesthetics. Imagination is central to Novalis's attempt to unify not only these diverse areas of human knowledge, but also the human self with nature. For imagination promised to unite what he considered the inner and outer sensibilities, or the inner life of the human mind with its perception of the world. Through imagination, the Romantics argued, our sense of the phenomenal and the transcendent, the natural and the divine, the scientific and the artistic will no longer be fragmented but will come together in the true intuition of life.



## Tragedy and the primal imagination

A harsh critic of Romantic thinkers and writers, Nietzsche thought their incessant yearning for the absolute nursed an unhealthy dissatisfaction with the world of our ordinary experience. Yet Nietzsche affirmed the deep interest in the imagination expressed by the Romantics, and considered the topic in several works. In an early essay, 'On Truth and Lies in an Extra-Moral Sense', Nietzsche defended the human imagination as a primal grasp of nature and condemned its subordination to conceptual knowledge. In *The Birth of Tragedy* (1872), Nietzsche put forth a naturalized aesthetic theory, in which tragic art is the expression of nature's creative imagination.

Nietzsche speculated on the origins of tragic poetry among the ancient Greeks, identifying what he calls the Apollonian and Dionysian drives. These—perhaps like imagination itself—are conceived as tendencies of nature expressed through the art 'without the mediation of the human artist'. Nietzsche invokes

Apollo as the god of the sun and light, order, beauty, and knowledge, as one who personifies reason, moderation, and moral virtue. The Apollonian would see reality as defined by stable, eternal, forms, epitomized by the idealizations of ancient Greek sculpture. Since Apollo is also the god of dreams—or oracular prophecy and visions—Nietzsche argues that the Apollonian vision is an illusion that hides the suffering and chaos underlying nature.

In contrast, the ancient Greeks associated Dionysus with music, intoxication, and sensuality. Nietzsche recounts the legends of the followers of Dionysus who revelled, in their rituals to the god, in drunken erotic dances and sometimes violent sacrifice. As such the Dionysian impulse represents chaotic mingling and fusion of beings, irrationality, and the boundlessness of chaos and constant change within nature. While the Apollonian art instinct produces beautiful appearances, the Dionysian unveils a violent, chaotic vitality.

Both drives, Nietzsche claims, are necessary for art. As an artform that involves spectacle or visual illusion (actors in masks on the stage), and musical poetry (the chorus was sung), tragic drama emerges from the agonistic tension between them. In a tragic age, and in great tragedies, the Dionysian impulse is fully manifest. In Nietzsche's account, the death of tragedy—and the suppression of the Dionysian insight—results from the advance of rationalist philosophy in ancient Greek society. Just as the tragic poets would be silenced by the Socrates of Plato's *Republic*, the play of imagination is suppressed by the oppressive domination of reason.

Nietzsche's essay 'On Truth and Lies in a Nonmoral Sense' (1873) challenges Plato's association of imagination with illusions and lies. The essay offers an account of the emergence of language and of the abstract structures of conceptual thought which in his view suppresses the more primal intuitions of imagination. In the essay Nietzsche argues that the repeated association of words and objects, and the generalizations necessary to construct concepts, diminish originally vivid and diverse perceptions that feed imaginative thought. In the emergence of conceptual ideas, the more original, imaginative experience of reality is diminished. Turning Plato's theory on its head, Nietzsche argues that rational thought constructs a false representation of reality at the expense of a more original, and more imaginative, experience.

The vital diversity within experience falls away when we communicate about it in words, in Nietzsche's view, just as the imprint from an ancient coin rubs off with repeated use. The word and concept for 'leaf', for example, necessarily abstract from the experiential diversity of leaves as experienced in nature. The necessary generalizations of the linguistic process lead us to think of the abstract idea of things as their essential truth, and their diverse manifestations are disregarded. While such a process of representation is necessary for higher cognition, the generalization involved, Nietzsche argues, eliminates the individuality and diversity of pre-conceptual experience.



Nietzsche may not have intended his essay to propose a serious theory of linguistic cognition, but rather concern that our evolved cognitive habits suppress the 'primal faculty of human imagination'. Some uses of language—such as poetry or lyrical music—will recover and promote imaginative thought. In referring to a 'stammering language' that might preserve our imaginative vivacity, Nietzsche seems to hold out the possibility that novel and creative uses of language may break with ordinary modes of conceptualization. Such would be the contribution of the artist or poet in restoring a more primal relation to the experienced world. This would involve what Nietzsche described as 'the return of language to the nature of imagery', recovering imagination in its interconnections with earthly life.

Modern thought might also become more imaginative, Nietzsche argued, by taking cues from philosophers who came before Plato.

In *Philosophy in the Tragic Age of the Greeks* Nietzsche described pre-Socratic philosophical thought as the expression of profound creative thinking. Ancient philosophers such as Thales identified primal elements, such as water, as the originating principles of all of being. Nietzsche describes the procedures of such thinking as 'propelled by an alien, illogical power—the power of creative imagination' as it leaps from possibility to possibility. In such thinking:

> Creative premonition will show the place; imagination guesses from afar that here it will find a demonstrable resting place. But the special strength of imagination is its lightning-quick seizure and illumination of analogies.

Here Nietzsche describes imaginative thinking as an intuitive prospecting for possibilities, through which process the mind may recognize and illuminate analogies, nurturing the eruption of new thoughts. In this analysis of cognition and in his tragic aesthetics, Nietzsche counts imagination as a vital human power and anticipates contemporary theories of creative cognition discussed in more detail in the final chapter of this book.

Imagination is involved in constituting our very experience of the world. It nurtures aesthetic experiences such as of beauty and the sublime. Yet we may also deliberately engage this capacity, in its free spontaneous play, to transform what is directly given in our experience. Productive imagination makes human creativity, and therefore human culture, possible.

Kant's acknowledgement of the productive imagination operating both in the constitution of experience and its aesthetic amplification provoked a radical affirmation of imagination by Romantic thinkers and writers. Imagination came to be understood as allowing the human mind to grasp what transcends direct experience, and to reconcile the mind with nature. Coleridge's attempt to understand imagination as both receptive and directed by our consciousness initiated a theory of creativity that will be influential in the following centuries. The Romantic view of imagination as unifying the inner life of the subject with the world is echoed, if radically transformed, in Nietzsche's affirmation of art and his call to an imaginative faculty more primal and vital than our conceptual representations of things.

In the next chapter we will explore the fascinating implications of the 'productive turn' as explored in 20th-century theories of imagination.

# Chapter 5
# The augmentation of reality

While imagination may contribute to the formation of experience, it also augments reality by endowing it with distinctly human meaning. The productive imagination celebrated by aesthetic philosophies of the 19th century and discussed in the previous chapter came to be explored in important philosophical movements in the 20th. In this chapter we will discuss how perception is inflected with and transformed by imagination through 'seeing-as', or interpretive perception. We will consider that imagination, though free from the constraints of reality, may also possibilize the real, or endow our sense of reality with possibility. We will turn to the means, including metaphor, narrative, political ideals, and scientific models, through which imagination is thought to generate new fictional meanings as well as new frameworks for understanding reality itself.

While hardly a divine creative power, seeing-as, first described by Wittgenstein, makes possible a human perspective on the world, and fosters imaginative expression. An important development in philosophy of imagination is its study by phenomenology, which attends to the structure of appearances to consciousness. While Sartre generally demarcated imagination strictly from perception—regarding perception as entirely separate from acts of imagination in the mind—he also acknowledged concrete imagining through which reality is imaginatively perceived and recognized in its latent possibilities. In Merleau-Ponty's studies of modern painting, this latency is regarded as an imaginative correlate of our embodied experience of the world. That is, through our experience of being an embodied subject moving in time and space among other things, we build up a repertoire of orientations and expectations which while not always fully given in direct perception are filled in and supplemented by imagination. Ricoeur shifted the philosophy of imagination from its focus on quasi-perceptual imaging to linguistic imagination, thus expanding the notion of productive imagination to account for the human ability to create new meaning. These 20th-century theories acknowledge the wide-ranging significance of imagination for the augmentation of reality in human perception, including the human encounter with a world perceived as meaningful.



## Seeing-as and aspect perception

In his *Philosophical Investigations* (1953), Wittgenstein described the ability to view something in one of multiple ways as seeing-as, or 'noticing an aspect', sometimes referred to as aspect perception. In this experience perception involves imagination as a presentational power (the word Wittgenstein often uses for imagination is *Vorstellung*). Wittgenstein's recognition of the involvement of imagination in perception owes much to the idea that the imagination may work productively. 'Seeing-as' expresses both the productivity and the spontaneity of the human mind and allows us to view the world around us as latent with significance. Unlike reproductive imagination, which only presents an object that was once experienced but is now absent to perception, seeing-as interprets or embellishes the perceptual presence of an object while and as it is seen.

In order to explain seeing-as, Wittgenstein states that we have to describe 'seeing' in two different ways. There is straightforward perceptual seeing, or taking in visual data, and a further kind of perceptual recognition through resemblance. He writes:

> Two uses of the word 'see'.
>
> The one: 'What do you see there?'—I see *this*' (and then a description, a drawing, a copy). The other: 'I see a likeness in these two faces'... What is important is the categorical difference between the two 'objects' of sight. I observe a face, and then suddenly notice its likeness to another. I see that it has not changed; and yet I see it differently. I call this experience 'noticing an aspect.'

The first kind of seeing is something like primary perception. The second kind of seeing, aspect perception or seeing-as, visually registers the same object in light of its resemblance to or association with another.

In the *Investigations*, Wittgenstein offers his now-famous example of an ambiguous puzzle picture: lines on a page make out the figure of a rabbit, or alternatively that of a duck (Figure 4). Without any other changes in the perceptual object or the conditions of its viewing, the viewer notices a shift in the aspect. The same lines on the page appear in one moment as the rabbit, in another as the duck, and the imaginative embellishment of perception, or its interpretive nature, becomes evident. The English philosopher P. F. Strawson pointed out that this change in aspect 'merely dramatizes for us a feature (namely seeing as) which is present in perception in general'. The implications of this capacity are profound, particularly when we consider the range of its manifestations.

Wittgenstein identified a variety of related phenomena as seeing-as. We see a human shape where there were previously branches. We see a horse in an unmoving picture as galloping. We see a triangle 'as a mountain, as a wedge, as an arrow or pointer'. In seeing-as, one thing is not only taken for something else.

**4. Ludwig Wittgenstein's 'Duck-Rabbit' in *Philosophical Investigations*.**



In pretence, children designate and treat the log *as if* it were a pirate ship. Yet in seeing-as, one thing is *seen as* something other through a particular quality. One thing is perceived in light of another.

In Chapter 2 the phenomenon of seeing star clusters as constellations was discussed. This involves a dual experience of perception and figuration: a group of stars may be seen both as points of light in the sky and, for example, as the hunter Orion. In such seeing-as, the visual perception is augmented by the simultaneous eliciting of a figurative potential. I can see stars straightforwardly as points of light among others, and also recognize them as making out the likeness, figure, image of another object. The perceptual object is not itself changed in the shift from bare seeing to seeing-as, but the experienced perception is altered. Since seeing-as is enabled by imagination, we might describe it as imaginatively endowed perception.

Yet seeing-as also accounts for our ability, further, to understand representations or make out visual reference. Looking at a sketch, we can 'see' the object it makes out—a human figure, for example—rather than first and foremost the lines and physical markings which construct the representation. Wittgenstein describes this phenomenon such that 'we regard the photograph, the picture on our wall, as the object itself (the man, landscape, and so on) depicted there'. Such perceptual interpretation generates a surplus beyond mere sense-perception in the form of an identification with or recognition of what is not strictly empirically given. Wittgenstein clarifies that such cases are not merely a matter of referential knowledge, but of a form of perception. The vehicle for meaning (the branches as human figure or the picture as the landscape) is experienced perceptually *as* that which it conveys. The phenomenological philosopher Husserl called this 'picture-consciousness', and it was analysed, alongside other forms of imaginative experience, in Sartre's study *The Imaginary*.



Seeing-as allows that, beyond grasping physical facts before us, we can view things as endowed with significance or meaning. We grasp not literal connections between things, but rather what Wittgenstein called their 'internal relations', such that our perception of the facts is transformed in a lived experience. These experiences of interpretive seeing are widespread across human perception, and are necessary for the perception of art and symbolic thinking, and can also lead to creative expression. Yet seeing-as remains in tension with the freedom from reality imagination is thought to endow.

## Phenomenology of mental imaging

If imagination can amplify or augment the perception of reality, it also works in sharp distinction from the real. In his major work of existentialist philosophy *Being and Nothingness* (1943), Sartre proposed that human consciousness is free because it is fundamentally distinct from the material world and can, in a sense, 'negate' it or its power over the mind. While everything else in reality has 'being', Sartre argues, consciousness is, rather, 'nothing', though it 'exists' as aware of itself and of whatever it is conscious of at any given moment. Imagination enables consciousness to distance itself from, and present alternatives to, reality. According to Sartre's philosophy, while physically I may be confined to a particular place and condition, in my mind I am free. This freedom reflects the fact that I can imagine the world differently from its actual existence and can imagine, too, elsewhere and otherwise than I directly experience.

This existential viewpoint also inflects Sartre's study *The Imaginary* (1940), which engages the practice of phenomenology, the first-person form of description mentioned in the first chapter of this book. Phenomenology allowed Sartre to defeat what he regarded as a crucial mistake in traditional accounts of imagination, namely the 'illusion of immanence', or the treatment of the mental image as if it were a thing or object in the mind. Sartre argues that the image is not an object, but a *way* of intending something not directly present to consciousness.



When we imagine something that is not present, this non-presence can take a number of forms. We can imagine something as elsewhere (to use Sartre's example, my friend Pierre in Berlin). We can imagine something as non-existent (e.g. a unicorn). We can imagine something as simply absent (a lion, wherever one may be). We can also imagine something without positing its existence or whereabouts at all (imagining something irrespective of its ontological or locational status). In terms of Sartre's own existentialism, imagination is at once constituting and negating, since it presents its object, but as a 'nothingness'. Images do not take up space in reality as do objects of perception, but inhabit what Sartre describes as an irreality—a phenomenal, experiential mode of presence to consciousness independent of reality itself. Because imagination allows us to consider any object as 'irreal', or in the mode of an image, it frees consciousness from the determinations of reality.

While rejecting the idea that the image is a thing in the mind, Sartre offers a phenomenological account of the process of inner visual imagining. The image is a way of being conscious of something, in a certain mode. When I am imagining something, he points out, the image is given or presented all at once, and therefore is not easily manipulatable: we cannot divide an image, seamlessly connect it with another, or render an already static image mobile. When imagining the Pantheon, I cannot easily count its columns, while perceiving the Pantheon I can accumulate detailed knowledge by inspecting it more closely, turning this way or that to accumulate a view of the whole. If I have an image of Pierre's head, I cannot add a top hat to it without its being merely pasted on—I can't invoke the 'look' Pierre would have wearing a top hat unless I replaced one image with another. I cannot make an imagined standing figure walk towards me except in a jerky, awkward way. Images are incomplete and ephemeral, and in this way, they are distinct from perceptions. When I supply further detail or transform an image, I have to in fact supply a new image to take its place. Contemporary theorists have taken up Sartre's interest in the manipulation of mental imagery in their defence of the relevance of mental imagery for studies of imagination. In *Image and Mind* (1980), Kosslyn pointed to such manipulation as support for the relevance of the mental image, which he continued to defend in later empirical studies, and it has served as the basis for Casey's phenomenological elaboration *Imagining* (2000).



While Sartre's description of inner envisioning is based largely on his own reflective experience, the human mind's imaging capacity is known to be variable. This variation was first proposed in 1880 by Francis Galton, who had conducted an informal survey of people asked to consider the nature of their experiences of imagining. Galton's study was recognized by William James in *Principles of Psychology* (1890), who appreciated that while some people have a remarkable facility to inwardly envision, others have poorer facilities. Failing to appreciate this difference, James argued, may lead to a 'false' view of imagination.

It is worth pausing here to consider this variation. There are, at one end of the spectrum, individuals who have extraordinary facilities of inner envisioning—what psychologists now call *hyperphantasia*, an exceptional capacity for complex visual detail. For example, the Serbian-American Nikola Tesla, inventor of the induction motor, invented in his mind before taking pen to paper. Tesla could mentally envision an invention down to the last measurements and all its moving parts, a process which enabled him to become extraordinarily prolific, with around 300 patents to his name. We can also point to novelist Vladimir Nabokov, who in his *Lectures on Russian Literature* (1981) advised his students to envision literary scenes in precise detail. When reading *Anna Karenina*, we ought to be able to see in which corner of the train carriage Anna is sitting, which direction she is facing, and what she can view from her seat—for which task Nabokov provided a diagram. On Kafka's *Metamorphosis* Nabokov supplied a drawing of the insect-like Gregor Samsa, despite the text itself leaving many details (such as how many legs Gregor has) indeterminate (Figure 5). For Nabokov it is the writer's 'vision' which the reader must enliven. At the other end of the spectrum, people with a condition called *aphantasia* cannot invoke visual images at all. James himself admitted to poor facility in visualization. Even highly literary minds may not engage inner envisioning. In *Fiction and the Figures of Life* (1970), William Gass, himself a novelist who had briefly studied with Wittgenstein, argued that fiction was not made from descriptions, but rather ideas.

In addition to wholly envisioned images, Sartre's phenomenology also takes up several different kinds of referential images—an 'image family'—of a photograph of a person, a portrait of a person, a schematic sketch of a person. While Wittgenstein included such images as instances of seeing-as, Sartre argues that in such cases we *perceive* the physical object—the photograph, the canvas and

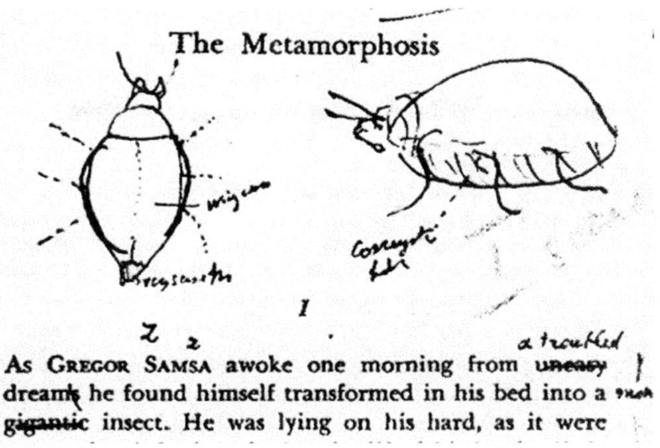


**5. Vladimir Nabokov's sketch of Gregor Samsa from Kafka's *The Metamorphosis*.**



paint, or the lines on a page—but we *imagine* the object it refers to. What we imagine is not the actual figure in the photograph (Pierre in the exact second it was taken) but the person it evokes. Sartre claims that a physical object serves as an 'analogon' for imagining. There is an implicit reliance here on the notion of resemblance, and thus on reproductive imagination—the photograph can serve as analogon for imagining since it resembles the person so imagined.

Sartre concedes that when, without a physical prompt such as a photograph or sketch, I simply imagine a person not present, the mind must have an 'analogon' too, but Sartre admits it is difficult to pin down what that may be. He suggests the motion of consciousness paying attention to the image, or the kinaesthetic sensations involved in the constitution of the image, and the affectivity wound up with it. Neuroscience has demonstrated that our visual imaging occurs in the same neuronal regions as does vision itself. Sartre's theory of the analogon may be difficult to square entirely with his thesis of the image as nothingness, if the analogon ends up positing something like a virtual schema in the mind produced by neurons. In other words, the image may not be strictly speaking 'nothing' but have a physical neurological correlate produced through imaginative acts of the mind.

## Revealing and 'possibilizing' reality

Sartre's theory, like that of Wittgenstein, does allow for a kind of interpretive perception. When we see, for example, a spot on the tablecloth as a particular figure, faces in the fire, or rocks seeming to make out a human form, Sartre posits that we pass into an imaginative attitude. I can perceive it as a spot and that is all, or I can 'pretend to "see" the image', or survey it in a certain way. While Sartre relies on pretence to maintain his distinction between imagining and perceiving, it may be that, when seeing lines on a page which are representative (as in an illustration or schematic drawing), this potentiality is incorporated in interpretive perception of the lines themselves.



This would be supported by Sartre's recognition of imagination's involvement in 'revealing' how the world appears to us. In this Sartre owed something to the work of the German philosopher Martin Heidegger, who in his work *Being and Time* had argued that the human being is involved in 'revealing' the world. Heidegger termed the human being 'Dasein', which means 'being-there' or 'being-here', in the sense of existing, thus emphasizing how concern for our own being defines us. The activities of imagination for Heidegger would be enactive, since we as Dasein reveal the world not because we put a picture of the world together in the mind, but because we interact with it according to our projects and concerns, in light of our attunements to it and of our own relation to possibilities.

On this view, the experienced world is not merely a totality synthesized by the mind, or a collection of material stuff, but a rich and vital realm of potentiality. Experiencing the world as latent with possibilities requires our being able to transcend or go beyond what is merely there and reveal it *as* something or in certain ways. Sartre takes up Heidegger's idea that we 'reveal' reality in these ways, but while Heidegger emphasizes practical concerns, for Sartre such revealing is explicitly imaginative. For Sartre it is through imagination that we lend our emotional and aesthetic values to what we see.

The idea that imagination reveals reality from a living point of view is also explored in the work of Merleau-Ponty, who emphasized embodied interaction as the basis from which we relate to and reveal possibilities. Through our embodied, interactive engagement of things, we relate to the prospects for action and perception we can undertake with them, a relationality which unfolds in time. In 'Eye and Mind' and other essays devoted to aesthetics, Merleau-Ponty interpreted the painting of Paul Cézanne as emblematic of embodied seeing. In Cézanne's paintings objects are rendered in modulations of colour and in trembling, overlapping outlines, and their distortions, more than any photographic likeness, capture the sense of living perception (Figure 6). Such painting, according to Merleau-Ponty, shows the world not merely as a set of brute facts, but as inviting our interaction through the potentialities we register. The potentiality that surrounds things is (Merleau-Ponty claims in his work *The Visible and the Invisible*) like a halo around the visible, 'a presence of the immanent, the latent, or the hidden' in the world before us that makes it rich with implicit meaning.

Sartre also wrote extensively about works of art and literature, and sometimes in this context associated imagination with what he called the 'possibilization' of reality. Since the function of imagination is to render whatever is to be imagined 'irreal', what is imagined can be varied in the mind towards other possible configurations. While Sartre emphasized the difference between the imagined and the perceived, he also thought that our sense of the world was enriched by this difference. We can augment our

**6. Paul Cézanne, *Still Life with Apples* (1890), The Hermitage, St Petersburg.**

understanding of the world as it is with possibilities afforded through imagination, and generate prospective alternatives.

While philosophers had recognized that our involvement with the world is necessary for our coherent or meaningful experience of it, Sartre adds that such involvement is also necessary for the experience of irreality, which he also termed the 'imaginary'. In order to recognize an image or imagined object as 'irreal'—or ontologically distinct from reality—the world that it surpasses must too be posited. We must be able to imagine the bounds of reality in order to be able to surpass them imaginatively. Sartre argues that:

> For consciousness to be able to imagine, it must be able to escape from the world by its very nature, it must be able to stand back from the world by its own efforts. In a word, it must be free.

Standing back from the world is likened by Sartre to taking an artistic perspective. Sartre compares this to the distance an impressionist painter would take from the canvas in order to 'bring out the whole "forest" or "white water lilies" from the multitude of little strokes they have placed on the canvas'. Even recognizing reality as reality implies an irreality from which it can be distinguished. Thus our very sense of reality as real 'implies a hidden reaching beyond towards the imaginary'.

Despite his segregation of imagination and reality, Sartre recognized that imagination can also offer to perception means to its aesthetic or other symbolic realization, a revealing of reality that at once augments it. Aesthetic, affective, or symbolic meaning may not change the bare perceptual features of the reality perceived, but inflects their interpretation, how they are experienced. A mountain may appear beautiful or sublime as well as lonely or majestic, a sunset can appear glorious. In her study of Sartre, the British philosopher Mary Warnock identified examples of such 'concrete' imagining in Sartre's own descriptions of experience. When the protagonist of Sartre's novel *Nausea* looks at the gnarled dark root of the tree and sees it as existence laid bare, he is concretely imagining, for in such moments the perception itself is laden with existential value. In *Being and Nothingness* Sartre also describes moments of perception where reality is revealed in light of values informed by a given project. For a subject intending to climb the mountain, the 'brute given' of its difficult slope is 'revealed as scalable or unscalable'. To the artist, in contrast, that valuation of scalability is irrelevant, and the mountain instead 'is manifested as beautiful or ugly'. In both cases of concrete imagining, a surplus of meaning, whether of practical or aesthetic value, is provided by imagination. Sartre seems to admit that this imaginative revealing of reality is a latent possibility across the whole life of perception. The amplification of experience by imagination is poignantly suggested at the end of *The Imaginary*. Sartre writes:

Imagination is not an empirical power added to the mind, it is the mind itself in so far as it is free; *every concrete situation of the mind in the world is pregnant with the imaginary*, in that it is always present as a way of going beyond the real.

## Metaphor and the generation of meaning

In order to fully appreciate the productive imagination, we must consider not only the envisioned mental image and the experiences of concrete imagining, but the imaginative work of language. Ricoeur's major writings, including *The Rule of Metaphor* (1975) and *Time and Narrative* (1983–5), along with unpublished lectures on imagination, present metaphor and narrative structure as manifesting productive imagination. These are thought to create new meanings and (virtual) worlds that go beyond and transcend reality.



A tragic drama, for example, presents a situation of life and action through narrative structure. This structure is informed, as Aristotle argued of tragedy, by knowledge not of events already occurred but of what could happen. Ricoeur brings Aristotle's insight further to argue that a literary work presents a new world, one which may provoke viewers or readers to consider anew their ordinary world. In contrast to classical treatments of literature, Ricoeur argues that this presentation exceeds mimesis or representation. Fictions are not the result wholly of reproductive imagination, but produce experiential worlds and ideas that did not exist before.

Ricoeur argues that while some imaginings may be described in reproductive terms, fictional objects cannot be wholly understood by reference to an original. There is no real Hamlet of which Shakespeare's character is a copy—no matter that several aspects of the character may be derived from what Shakespeare previously experienced or knew. The fictional Hamlet is a dual reference both to the real world of familiar things—princes, sons—and to a fictional world which supersedes that reality, since we are not to take Hamlet as a real person but as a character. Ricoeur describes the creative effect of imagination as 'productive reference', highlighting the original ontological status of creative imaginings.

In order to promote the productive imagination against a merely reproductive view, Ricoeur reorients the philosophical understanding of fiction in two ways. Firstly, Ricoeur turns to the image conjured in language rather than that evoking perception. Plato, we recall, compares the images conjured by the poet to what he regards as the visual copies of things made by the painter; the painter and poet both 'copy' what they perceive. Ricoeur aims to demonstrate the insufficiency of conceiving the imagination as making a copy from perception. Such theories regard physically or linguistically created images, as well as those of inner fantasizing, as resemblances of the thing represented. For example, in Hume's view, images derive from and are copies of perceptions, or, in Sartre's view, they resemble absent objects of perception. Either way, Ricoeur thinks, images are treated as derivative. Yet according to Ricoeur, the image is not only a faded perception or resemblance but an emerging, original meaning.

Ricoeur, secondly, shifts the discussion from describing the isolated image to the elaboration across images of imaginative experience. This happens, for example, in metaphor, when two or more things are compared. Such elaboration also occurs in the narrative shaping of fictional works that produces a world or nexus of interrelated meanings through imaginatively unfolding action. Both according to Ricoeur involve the creation of new meaning.

According to Ricoeur, metaphor enables semantic innovation. In metaphor one thing is not merely named as another, but is given predicates or qualities normally reserved for something different. With 'all the world's a stage', Shakespeare compared life to a dramatic performance. The American poet Robert Frost compared life to making one's way in the woods. In his poem 'Birches', for example, Frost's speaker complains of a moment when 'life is too much like a pathless wood' and dreams of leaving it just for a while to begin anew. In 'The Road Less Travelled' Frost's speaker tells of taking the less-worn of two paths 'and that has made all the difference'. In such examples, metaphor synthesizes two different meanings and yet maintains the old pertinence along with the new. Life is not strictly speaking a stage or a path through the woods, but again the resonances within these couplings make us think of life in new ways. In metaphoric coupling likeness is perceived across the unlikeness, and a new spark of meaning originates. Rather than merely a tarnished and faded percept of reality, the metaphoric image, Ricoeur suggests, emerges as a nascent signification.

While drawing on Aristotle and Kant in his elaboration of the productive imagination, Ricoeur also finds inspiration in the French philosopher Gaston Bachelard's phenomenological study of poetic imagery, *The Poetics of Space*. In this work, Bachelard treats poetic images as generators of meaning that draw from early embodied experiences of life. Bachelard's study focuses on spatial images, for example spaces of shelter, or open expanses of exploration. The image of a path through woods from Frost's poem would resonate with early experiences of making one's way home from the wide world. Such images do not merely mimic or represent spaces in the world, but also resonate with the reader's embodied memory. Adapting a term to his phenomenology of poetic imagery, Bachelard argues that such images 'reverberate' in the imagination, as evoked memory and new meaning are together awakened in the reader's mind.

Beyond metaphor, language also generates new meaning through narrative. In reading literary fiction, images are formed through the metaphoric evocation and display of relations. As readers of a novel, we are provoked to evoke an experiential world. As we do so, dormant memories may be awakened, similar experiences reanimated, but imagination radiates further and gives shape to a new experience in a free play of possibilities mediated by language. In contrast to Nabokov's descriptions of literary reading, literary imagining for Ricoeur is not strictly speaking a form of seeing something in the mind, but rather of apprehending a meaning alluded to in a play of related images through which emerges a fictional world.

The idea that the productive imagination augments our sense of reality can be illustrated with reference to artistic expression. Whether in writing or painting, imagination does not only represent elements of reality but performs what Ricoeur calls an 'iconic augmentation' of them. An artistic presentation can transform what it presents, for example through abridging and condensing its subject matter, and through this a surplus meaning arises. A landscape—for example, Vincent van Gogh's *Starry Night*—frames a particular point of view, and intensifies through colour, line, brushstroke, and composition the relations among the elements presented there. Such framing and intensification may occur in a poem through the play of verbal imagery. What is thereby imagined in each case is more than what is merely there.



Such surplus meaning also illuminates the ordinary world in a new way. Wallace Stevens described in similar terms the creative augmentation of our sense of things. He described a poem as:

> a particular of life thought of for so long that one's thought has become an inseparable part of it or a particular of life so intensely felt that the feeling has entered into it.

This kind of mental poetry can and does become the stuff of life experience. When we see or even merely think of a blue sky, for example, it is not merely visual or quasi-visual data but evokes a sense of the warmth of sunshine, an absence of troubling storms, new chances, limitless prospects, or even happiness. In this way the geography of the world is informed by the 'non-geography' of our imagination. Stevens expands:

> when, by way of illustration, we cite, say, the blue sky, we can be sure that the feeling has become a part of our vital experience of life, even though we are not aware of it.

Related to Wittgenstein's sense of seeing-as and to Sartre's notion of concrete imaging, this effect of productive imagination is an augmentation of our sense of things, of the reality we live. It is an expansion of our being-in-the-world, as existentialist philosophers refer to the lived world with which we meaningfully interact and through which our existence is elaborated.



Imagination is productive not only in literature and art but in many domains of human thought and life. Ricoeur describes political utopias, for example, as productive fictions, since they project ideal states which do not yet exist. Benedict Anderson argued in *Imagined Communities* (1983) that nationalistic sensibilities are constructed imaginatively across a society as individuals imagine themselves as a part of a distinct social group. Such constructions can be dangerous if unrestrained. For as the German-Jewish philosopher Hannah Arendt argued in *The Origins of Totalitarianism* (1951), the subject of totalitarianism has lost the distinctions between fiction and fact, truth and falsity. At the same time moral freedom, she noted, also requires imagination—by creating reflective distance from immediate experience, such that we can consider potential actions.

The imagination's use in the attainment of scientific knowledge also bears some comparison with its generation of meaning in other contexts. Through the generation of theoretical models, Ricoeur argues, scientists jettison old descriptions of reality in order to redescribe it with heuristic metaphor. Some examples of such scientific modelling include Thomas Young's representation of light as waves rather than particles, or James Clerk Maxwell's understanding of an electrical field in terms of fluidity. While such models aim to capture the nature of reality, they are ways of redescribing it. According to François Jacob, such models are in some ways comparable to innovative artworks. He argues that it is by undoing a perceived reality 'in order to remake it differently that the painter, the poet, or the scientist builds up a vision of the universe'.

The elaboration of the productive imagination transformed the philosophy of imagination and preoccupied philosophers throughout the 20th century. From Wittgenstein's study of seeing-as we can recognize imagination at work in symbolic and interpretive perception and expression. While describing the negating power of imagining in distinction from reality, Sartre nevertheless recognized its productive contribution to experience, and highlighted the freedom of imagination to reveal reality. Just as Sartre describes imagination's possibilization of the real, Ricoeur described its augmentation through metaphor. Merleau-Ponty's studies of painting and Bachelard's of poetic imagery both engage phenomenology to illuminate how imagination augments our reception of reality. Whether in service to knowledge, rendering landscapes, or generating fictional worlds, amplifications of productive imagination are found across many modes of human thought and action. The productive imagination and its role in human thinking will be central to understanding creativity, on which we will focus in the next chapter.

# Chapter 6
# Creativity from invention to wonder

Nowhere is productive imagination more visible than in creativity, where multiple modes of imagination may be put to work to generate novel, meaningful, and useful ideas. Through creativity we integrate imagination with the world around us, taking up material objects, sounds, language, or existing ideas to forge something new. Though the skills of ordinary thinking may be involved, creativity does not follow its habitual grooves, but leaps unpredictably. Creativity is essential (not only in the arts but also in science) for solving problems and enhancing our everyday lives.

While philosophers have long considered creativity as part of aesthetics, in recent decades it has been studied as a more fundamental aspect of cognition. At the same time, interest in creativity has exploded in the human sciences. Yet neither philosophers nor scientists have fully explained creativity, which eludes logical or mechanistic explanation and may be difficult to fully replicate in a laboratory. To better understand creativity, it may help to consider its flourishing in the context of our being-in-the-world, the way in which we engage with our surrounding world by transforming it, and in light of the interconnections between reality and possibility.

In this chapter we will take a closer look at creativity as a means of negotiating reality through imagination, finding insight in sources from ancient philosophy to contemporary cognitive theory. We will consider creativity's relation to imagination: its striving to overcome limitations and invest reality with possibilities. We will address inspiration and the role of cognitive play in creative thinking, and consider the roles of 'negative capability'—or the ability to proceed in uncertainty—curiosity, and wonder in nurturing creative life.

## From flights of fancy to creative invention

Creativity has long been associated with metaphors of flight and ascension, and with this we can consider creativity's relation to the human imagination. In his poem 'I Wandered Lonely as a Cloud' (1807) Wordsworth described his poetic imagination as viewing the world from above, able to take in a few of 10,000 daffodils in a 'never ending line' along a bay. The Irish poet William Butler Yeats referred to 'the balloon of the mind'. If imagination soars in flights of fancy, with creativity we may strive to make that real.

An ancient Greek myth recounted in Ovid's *Metamorphoses* (8 CE) illustrates this striving. Ovid tells of the master craftsman Daedalus imprisoned with his son Icarus in a labyrinth of his own design by the king of Crete. As their means of escape Daedalus created pairs of wings from wax and feathers. Ovid's account refers to onlookers—a ploughman, an angler, and a shepherd—who 'stood there amazed, believing them to be gods able to travel the sky'. Yet Icarus ignored his father's advice not to fly too close to the sun, fell into the sea, and drowned as the wax melted and the water weighed down his wings. The myth warns against hubris. But it also illustrates the human creative drive to surpass limitations, to transform reality or our perspective on it.

Icarus' fate was depicted with tragic if playful irony by the Dutch painter Pieter Brueghel (the Elder). His *Landscape with the Fall of Icarus* (c.1560) shows a glorious seascape with ships floating peacefully, with the ploughman and angler going about their

**7. Pieter Brueghel the Elder, *Landscape with the Fall of Icarus* (*c.*1560), Royal Museums of Fine Arts of Belgium, Brussels.**



work, the shepherd staring up at the sky, no one taking any notice of a pair of legs splashing in the water (Figure 7). Only Brueghel's viewers notice Icarus, for to make sense of the painting's title, they must fill in the narrative, create their own image of the fateful plunge. They are invited to imagine Icarus and his view on the world from above, the irresistible if ultimately fatal thrill of his ascension. Brueghel's painting about the perils of ambitious creativity speaks back to and stimulates the viewer's own imagination.

Just around the time Brueghel made his Icarus painting, the explorer Pedro Ceza de León published his *Chronicle of Peru* (1553), noting on the coastal plains peculiar trail markings that were later taken to be the remains of ancient roads. We now know them as the Nazca lines or geoglyphs, monumental works carved between 200 BCE and 500 CE. The lines make out hundreds of massive figures, including a hummingbird, monkey, lizard, spider, whale, llama, and tree, a pelican spanning 285 feet, and geometric designs as large as 1,200 feet. These were first seen from above in

**8. The spider, one of the geoglyphs made in the Nazca Desert in Southern Peru between 200 BCE and 500 CE by the Nazca people.**



1927 when rediscovered by Peruvian pilots. What is most striking about them is that their giant figures can be viewed fully only from the sky (Figure 8).

The Nazca geoglyphs may have served a practical purpose, such as outlining walking routes for the collection of water or constructing work areas for making rope or nets. The works may have been meant as religious communication to the gods of their creators. The works materially manifest creative imagining, for without airborne vessels to view them from above, the creators of these works would have had to imagine an aerial perspective of the figures the lines would make out. The Nazca figurations would have had to be mentally projected as they were worked onto the earth, illustrating creativity as a dynamic exchange between human consciousness and the physical world.

Early in the sixteenth century Leonardo da Vinci composed his notebooks, consisting of many thousands of pages of drawings that record among other things ideas for inventions and plans to make them into reality. With apparently tireless fascination, Leonardo studied, among many other things, the flight of birds, bats, and insects, alongside human anatomy, and combined his findings in designs for flying machines, such as the ornithopter and helicopter. While among these only his parachute and hang-glider designs have been built successfully, Leonardo's ideas were centuries ahead of his time, and are now seen to anticipate contemporary biomimetic design. They instigate what would become the history of human flight, advanced by the Montgolfier brothers' hot-air balloon transport (1783), the Wright Brothers' first human-occupied powered flight (1903), and travel to the moon in Apollo 11 by Neil Armstrong and Buzz Aldrin (1969).



While these inventions may all align with pragmatic aims, creativity may be wholly free of practical purpose, pursued solely for its own exercise. In 1974 Philippe Petit famously walked unaided between the towers of the World Trade Center on a tightrope 1,350 feet (411 metres) above the ground. The high-wire performance artist described feeling overpowered by the sky, venturing into a voluptuous unknown. With this singular event, the subject of many films and books, Petit accomplished what had theretofore seemed impossible and inspired a proliferation of creative reflections. His performance reflects our human drive to explore possibilities for their own sake and to integrate them into reality.

These examples may all illustrate an ancient human dream. The desire to transcend limitations, to rise above the world, and view it as we imagine a god might see it may have been first stirred for early humans recording the positions of stars on a cave wall. These feats also demonstrate creativity as facilitating a shift in our human perspective, enabling what Sartre called the 'possibilization' of the world we experience. It may be said that in each act of creation, a new and meaningful idea is generated by combining previous ideas—wax and feathers, figurative shapes and monumental geography, birds' flight and human anatomy, a walking human and the height of skyscrapers. Yet well beyond mere combination, these creative works integrate possibility into a lived human experience, to transform a given state of reality and expand our sense of what is possible.

## Inspiration and genius

How is such creativity inspired? Creative inspiration has long puzzled the artists, scientists, and inventors who depend on it and the philosophers who have attempted to explain it. For several thousand years inspiration was attributed to mystical sources received by the creative subject. Ancient Hindu texts include prayers for inspiration to Saraswati, the goddess of knowledge, music, and the arts. The ancient Greeks referred to the nine Muses as sources of human creativity, thought to inspire not only poets but also scientists and mathematicians. Their influence may be thought to involve a kind of possession. In Plato's dialogue *Ion*, Socrates describes the poet as 'unable to create until he [*sic*] becomes inspired and frenzied, his mind no longer in him'. Socrates argued that no one 'can compose or chant or prophesy' if they are not so possessed.

While eschewing much of its religious connotations, today's popular conception of creativity still echoes the ancient view of inspiration as a sudden flash of insight, a 'eureka' moment. That description of the creative moment comes from the legend surrounding Archimedes, a 3rd-century Syracusan, discovering a key to the principle of buoyant force. As author of many inventions such as the hydraulic screw, Archimedes had been asked by King Hiero to determine whether a crown was made with an admixture of inferior metals. Sitting in the baths, a solution suddenly dawned on Archimedes: that he could compare the density of objects through their respective displacement of water. He leapt from the baths shouting 'eureka!' or 'I have found [it]!' It is hard to know whether this legend recorded by the architect Vitruvius two centuries after Archimedes' death bears any historical truth. Yet it is reasonable to surmise that such solutions as Archimedes sought emerged in recognition of an analogy between distinct ideas simultaneously considered.

We might better understand creativity by acknowledging the lived context in which it emerges, or creativity as 'situated transcendence' as I termed it in *The Life of Imagination* (2018). For creativity emerges from and transforms a lived experiential situation that involves a whole cognitive ecology, or embodied, enactive situation in which the cognitive experience occurs. Although Vitruvius partly attributes Archimedes' inspiration to the Muses (as was conventional), he also points out that the inventor had spent many years in mathematical contemplation. The mathematician had frequently applied his expertise to the surrounding world—from figuring out how to best strengthen the city walls against invasion to attempting to reckon how many grains of sand might fit into the known universe. More than merely putting two ideas together, Archimedes in the eureka moment would have been stimulated by a physical context in which he considered his problem—his body submerging in water sparking an analogous recognition—along with a wide background of knowledge from different domains and a long-practised habit of problem-solving. The eureka moment, though apparently arising from nowhere, in fact arises from a whole cognitive ecology conducive to creative thought.



While the view of inspiration as a sudden flash from nowhere persisted for a long time in Western thought, by the 18th century, philosophers began to resist the convention of attributing artists' inspiration to an external source. Although in *Critique of Judgment* he described the artistic genius as the 'mouthpiece of nature', Kant also thought that the artist must attend to natural objects of beauty and attempt to create works based on their form through laborious practice.

> Hence this form is not, as it were, a matter of inspiration or of a free momentum of the mental powers; the artist is, instead, slowly and rather painstakingly touching the form up in an attempt to make it adequate to his thought while yet keeping it from interfering with the freedom in the play of these powers.

The genius is one who, giving expression to nature, can create exemplary works through gradual improvement. Kant recognized that this requires a particular exercise of cognitive faculties, balancing freedom and form through cognitive play.

It is striking that, according to Kant, genius cannot be wholly explained or consciously controlled. The genius 'cannot describe or indicate scientifically how it brings about its products', for the creator 'does not know how he [*sic*] came by the ideas for it; nor is it in his [*sic*] power to devise such products...or by following a plan, and to communicate...to others in precepts that would enable them to bring about like products'. Inspired genius, Kant thought, does not follow a formula, and cannot be taught.



## Everyday and exceptional creativity

While Kant is referring to exemplary creativity, the same faculties may be at work in everyday creativity, as 20th-century theorists of cognition began to recognize. In *Art as Experience* (1934), the American philosopher John Dewey described how the human propensity to creativity shapes our perceptions and arises from ordinary everyday life. Through creativity, Dewey argued, human beings express our need to make '*an* experience' that is 'unified and total' out of the flow of experience in general. For example, through religious rituals, preparing special meals, designing gardens, planning travel adventures, giving toasts, or celebratory events, we shape experiences that stand out and are distinguished from the ordinary flow of life. This occurs through variation from ordinary habits as well as the imposition of new constraints that work to shape experiences.

The arts express a more refined channelling and curating of this everyday creativity. For example, rather than flowing unrestricted and randomly, sound is given temporal and tonal structure through music, and thereby distinguished from the background noise. Through painting, colour and shape and visual detail are made to stand out from visual perception in general. In dance, movement of the human body is cultivated. In literature, we not only communicate with words but thereby conjure imagined worlds. Such creativity enhances and curates the processes of everyday life.



The idea that creativity is not an extraordinary phenomenon but continuous with everyday thinking was further pursued by Arthur Koestler in *The Act of Creation* (1964). Examining experiences ranging from the arts and sciences to telling jokes, Koestler argued that 'bisociation is the essence of creativity', in that it brings together different frameworks of thinking, cognitive skills, or patterns of rule-governed thought or activity in a sudden fusion. Koestler described creativity as the connective association of ideas from two unrelated matrices of thought, creating a new matrix. This process could involve comparing matrices, abstracting elements from them, categorizing them, or drawing analogies and metaphors between them.

Creativity has been identified as the very core of human cognition. Building on Koestler's theory, Giles Fauconnier and Mark Turner, in *The Way We Think* (2002), proposed to explain creativity through the notion of 'conceptual blending'. According to this theory the mind comes up with new ideas by blending two disparate concepts together in a third mental space of application. On this view, Archimedes would have integrated distinct concepts (themselves results of conceptual blends): displacement of water by the body and the relation of one metal to the mass of the whole, projected onto the new mental 'space' of the crown to be assessed. Yet the theory holds that conceptual blending or integration occurs not only in the conscious efforts of heightened creativity, but as an unconscious process underlying all human thinking.

Other theorists have argued that human thinking is intrinsically creative because it relies upon resources that go beyond logical or empirical comparison. As discussed in the previous chapter, metaphor allows for the creation of meanings irreducible to the elements of comparison. For Ricoeur, metaphor expresses the productive imagination and operates not only in literary and artistic works, but in scientific models and political theory. Yet metaphor may form a dimension of everyday thinking as well. In their works *Metaphors We Live By* (1980) and *Philosophy in the Flesh* (1999), George Lakoff and Mark Johnson argue that metaphor arises in transference from primal bodily experiences (such as feeling 'up' or 'down', 'warm' or 'cold', 'balanced' or 'imbalanced'), and that such primal metaphors give rise to conceptual thinking. In *Surfaces and Essences: Analogy as the Fuel and Fire of Thinking* (2013), the cognitive theorist Douglas Hofstadter and the psychologist Emmanuel Sander argue for the ubiquity of analogy-making within human thought, rejecting the relegation of this skill to relatively rare creative moments. Competing if also resonating with conceptual blending and metaphor-based cognitive theories, Hofstadter and Sander propose analogy as the origin of creativity.

Such theories are valuable in helping to demonstrate how our capacity for innovation expresses an intrinsic feature of the human mind. They suggest that creativity, rather than arriving from a mysterious external source, draws upon facilities that characterize human thinking in general. Yet taken alone such theories may leave important aspects of creative experience unexplained. The recognition of creativity as fundamental to human consciousness does not explain, for example, the proliferation of prospective conceptual blends, metaphors, or analogies in exceptional creativity, or illuminate how this facility comes to be elaborated and directed by some imagining minds but not by others. It remains to be understood how particularly meaningful or innovative new combinations or analogies are distinguished from the potentially random flow of blends, metaphors, or analogies. Such theories also leave unexplained how creativity may direct thought against the grain of cognitive habit. Creativity even in the sciences requires deviation from standard ways of thinking, involving acceptance of risk and potential failure. These go beyond combinational or even metaphorical mechanics and entail attitudes and dispositions that may be emotive and existential in nature.

While creative inspiration appears to evade direct analysis, psychological research has revealed some of the conditions that may nurture creativity. The creativity of young children appears to thrive in relative naivety, declining in adolescence with the refinement of higher reasoning and the acquisition of knowledge. Among adults, in contrast, a wide basis of knowledge is beneficial for creativity, since it supplies ideas from which to make new and meaningful combinations. Further, cross-training or input of ideas from different fields is recognized as a promoter of creativity, enhancing the generation of new useful or meaningful combinations. The fields from which creativity draws may be very far apart. Einstein, for example, claimed that the 'combinatory play' that led to new scientific insights was stimulated when he played the violin. While Kant's view that practice and its 'process of improvement' assist creative production has been substantiated, studies show that over-practice, or an excess of repetition, may stifle it.

One aspect of creativity that has puzzled researchers is its relation to freedom and constraint. Despite his respect for disciplined practice on the part of the genius, the free play of the imagination in aesthetic experience is an important part of Kant's aesthetic theory. The association of imagination with freedom appears to be echoed in Kant's view that the genius can neither explain nor conduct the process of inspiration. Sartre emphasized the imagination's freedom from all worldly circumstances. As free and unformulaic, creativity is spontaneous. One might imagine the creator beginning with a blank page, with no constraints at all on a given project. At the same time, creative thinkers themselves have testified that constraint tends to encourage creativity rather than diminish it.

For example, while modernist avant-garde artists broke with accepted tradition, throwing out many accepted conventions, they also praised the virtues of some formal limitations for creating new works. The French poet Charles Baudelaire revolutionized poetry by rejecting romantic descriptions of beautiful nature and instead turning to the outcasts and refuse of modern urban Paris for his themes. In his revolutionary collection *Les Fleurs du mal* (*Flowers of Evil*) (1857), he described the creative yearning in a poem as a kind of voyage to plumb 'the bottom of the Unknown in order to find something new'. Yet in his essay 'The Salon of 1859', Baudelaire also advised artists not to venture haphazardly away from traditional form. Rules for the production of art, he claimed, 'have assisted the birth of originality', as they respect the human need for some sense of order. Baudelaire thought that the restrictiveness of the formal sonnet, for example, could intensify the bursting forth of an idea.

Similarly, Robert Frost warned of the modern poet's tendency to follow arbitrary associations, leading to mere abstraction from life and inconsequential associations. In 'The Figure a Poem Makes', Frost warned of 'giving way to undirected associations and kicking ourselves from one chance suggestion to another in all directions' like a grasshopper on a hot afternoon. On Frost's view, poetry is most fulfilling when it offers 'a momentary stay against confusion' and this may be aided by aspects of form which are not only restrictive but generative. Of poetic metre, for example, Frost advises that: 'The possibilities for tune from the dramatic tones of meaning struck across the rigidity of a limited metre are endless.'

The Russian composer Igor Stravinsky also praised constraint as necessary for art, despite his own radical contributions to avant-garde music. In his *Poetics of Music* (1942), Stravinsky claimed that:

> The more that art is controlled, limited, worked over, the more it is free... In art as in everything else, one can build only upon a resisting foundation: whatever constantly gives way to pressure, constantly renders movement impossible... My freedom thus consists in my moving about within the narrow frame that I have assigned to myself for each one of my undertakings...

Stravinsky's respect for creative constraint is all the more striking when we consider the intensity of his innovations in modern music. His ballet *The Rite of Spring* provoked a riot at its 1913 premiere in Paris. The audience was scandalized not only by the jerky, awkward, or erotic movements of the dancers of Diaghilev's Ballets Russes but by the harsh primitivist sounds and the intense dissonance of the score. T. S. Eliot wrote of Stravinsky's work that he had made music from the 'barbaric cries of modern life' and its 'despairing noises'.

Jazz music, based on unscripted improvisation, perhaps best epitomizes the play between freedom and constraint in creative thinking. Jazz, traditionally dispensing with reliance on written scores, historically emerged from an early 20th-century black American culture striving for freedom from societal oppression, and is thus culturally as well as artistically associated with freedom. In discussing jazz, which served as the motif for her novel of that title, Toni Morrison wrote that 'imagination fosters real possibilities'. Yet despite its innovative freedom, the improvisation fundamental to jazz relies upon established practice, mastery of techniques, and deviation from standards long familiar. Improvisational performance is enabled by its characteristic call and response among musicians, who inspire one another by generating an ongoing collaborative framework for innovative nuance, unfolding in real time.

Advances within the jazz genre can also illuminate the relationship between freedom and the constraints of artistic foundations. With his album *Kind of Blue* (1959), Miles Davis advanced a new musical direction, that of modal jazz. Working with the music theorist George Russell, Davis shifted the basis for improvisation from chord changes to scales or modes. Combinations were almost limitless, allowing for extraordinarily inventive expression. Yet the expansive freedom invoked by modal jazz was enabled by the new parameters—playing 'in the sound' of a given set of scales, as the album's pianist Bill Evans formulated it. *Kind of Blue* catalysed the evolution of jazz music and is regularly cited as the most successful jazz album ever recorded.

## Cognitive play

The collaboration of freedom and form, standard practice and innovation that characterizes jazz music is captured in the notion of cognitive play, about which we can find some insight from aesthetic theory. Like much insight into imagination, the notion of cognitive play first came to prominence with Kant's aesthetics. We have seen that for Kant, artistic creativity along with receptive aesthetic experience involves the free play of cognitive powers. This idea was expanded by the German writer Friedrich Schiller towards a theory of the creative impulse of the human mind, or a theory of play. In his work *On the Aesthetic Education of Man in a Series of Letters* (1795), Schiller adapts Kant's ideas towards a social aesthetic of play.

Schiller suggests that human activity is directed by three interrelated instincts or 'drives', those of sense, form, and play. Schiller understands the modern human spirit as suffering an opposition between sense and form—or between intuition of the material, changing temporal world, and the formal measure associated with timeless laws. Schiller argues that the specialized rationality of modern life has fractured the 'inner unity of human nature', thus alienating these orientations from each other. Unchecked, the intuitive and free imagination squanders the fruits of rational thinking, while the abstract tendencies of understanding stifle imaginative vitality.

In play, however, these impulses come together in dynamic and productive activity. What Schiller calls the 'play drive' allows for a unification of these diverging orientations. Play generates 'living form' as we may find expressed in dynamic aesthetic experiences. As examples we might now think of the open choreography of modern dance, the improvisational play of jazz, interactive theatre, or imaginative children's play with surrounding objects as examples of reconciling sensuous or material spontaneity with the need for form. In *Aesthetic Education*, Schiller claims that it is 'precisely play and play alone, which in every human condition makes human beings whole and unfolds both sides of their nature at once'. Anticipating Winnicott's thesis on the necessity of play for a true sense of oneself, Schiller argued that play is the basis for a unified self, and makes us fully human.

The concept of play was further developed by the German philosopher Hans-Georg Gadamer. In his *Truth and Method* (1960), Gadamer conceives play as a relation between an activity and its participants (a game and its players, for instance), that is undertaken for its own sake, and manifests as a phenomenon that can be shared. In this sense, play is not simply a subjective enjoyment but a communicative activity. Since it takes shape through a manifest or objective event, play in this sense is equivalent to expressive creativity.

While creative play makes us most human, it also connects us with nature. In creative play we freely take up the stuff and experience of the material world and give it shape or form. Gadamer likens human play, including the play of words in literature, to the appearance of play in nature, such as the play of light, of waves, or of wind in the trees. Both human and elemental play are conceived as primal movements of energy. Human play is neither merely subjective (taking place wholly in the mind of the individual) nor wholly objective, but a living worldly exchange. Echoing Dewey's theory of art as the demarcation of *an* experience from its general flow, play as such becomes *a* play when its energy is shaped by form to create a representation for others.

Like play more generally, cognitive play entails both freedom and constraint, spontaneity and work, fluidity and form, while exposing new prospective directions for creative thought. The idea of cognitive play is important for understanding why neither knowledge nor practice, while important, are sufficient in themselves to ensure the generation of creative ideas. It also indicates why creativity is not only a matter of combining old ideas, but requires shifting the grooves of ordinary ways of thinking. When contemporary cognitive theorists try to explain creativity as a combinatory process, they tend to acknowledge randomness or chance as an element in the emergence of fruitful ideas. Yet it may be that cognitive play encourages the occasion of new prospects, for which the mind must be both open to and able to elaborate valuable, unexpected potentialities.



## Negative capability, defamiliarization, curiosity, and wonder

Creativity consists not only of combinatory cognitive skill, but also requires a disposition of openness to possibility and an elaborative engagement of a given context. Through cognitive play, creativity invites new ideas that may, in turn, also shift our perspective on what we know. This entails that, in order to be creative, we must be tolerant of, or even invite, the cognitive or aesthetic discord new ideas introduce, which may expose existing knowledge or practices as incomplete, limited, or in need of revision. While creativity can benefit from wide or deep knowledge and from formal or material constraints, it also requires tolerance for unknowing, for that which lies beyond expectation or the grasp of established knowledge or practice.

This crucial aspect of creativity was famously addressed in the English poet John Keats's notion of 'negative capability', which he defined as the ability, necessary for creative genius, to abide in 'uncertainties, mysteries, and doubts'. Keats found a model of negative capability in Shakespeare, in that the writer's expansive examination of human experience was undertaken with explorative depth and in acceptance of ambiguities not fully understood. In contrast, Keats chided the more established poet Coleridge for looking too much to philosophy for a universal certainty. Keats charged that one could not be open to discovery if one were 'incapable of remaining content with half-knowledge'. Too-fixed ideas were, he thought, incompatible with aesthetic experience. The wonder one might take in beauty, for example, did not demand explanation, for it 'overcomes every other consideration, or rather obliterates all consideration'.



For Keats negative capability meant, further, suspending the need for rationalization or factual verification, ceasing to appropriate the world to one's own established idea of truth, in favour of an intensely empathetic and varied perception. This may mean upsetting habitual perception and its assumptions, and an openness to surprising influences. We might find a visual illustration in van Gogh's *Starry Night* (1889), in which the artist depicted the summer skyscape above a Provençal town. In the previous chapter we referred to how a painting of a landscape might enable 'iconic augmentation' of its subject matter, a generation of meaning achieved through abridgement, or selection of the boundaries of the frame, and condensation, or intensification of the relations within it. We can see this in how van Gogh's work, with visionary empathy, depicts the stars in vital

**9. Vincent van Gogh, *The Starry Night* (1889), Museum of Modern Art, New York.**

and explosive movement, the moon in riotous glow (Figure 9). The sky appears as if communing with a human habitation almost swallowed up by nature in the form of undulating fields and cypress trees curling upward like dark flames. Merleau-Ponty thought that van Gogh's work showed how life is 'not shut up in the depths of the mute individual but diffused through all he sees'. At the time of its composition, the painting was a radical departure from conventional artistic representation of nature, and its first viewers found it unsettling.

The large morning star depicted in the painting represents what van Gogh could see from his asylum window where he temporarily resided towards the end of his life. Yet with its wave-like cloud currents and rolling fields, the painting may have also been inspired by the Japanese artist Katsushika Hokusai, in whose book of colour prints—including the famous *The Great Wave Off*

**10. Katsushika Hokusai, *The Great Wave off Kanagawa*, woodblock print from *Thirty-Six Views of Mount Fuji* (1831).**



*Kanagawa* (*c*.1829–33)—van Gogh had taken a keen interest. Van Gogh shaped his vision of the sky cresting over the hills with the same intense motility as Hokusai's magnificently curving wave, which threatens to overwhelm boats in the Sagami Bay and dwarfs Mount Fuji (Figure 10). Among many aspects of van Gogh's accomplishment was his recognition in the skies above not of a cold and distant otherworldly space or a distance as would be measured by astronomers, but of fluid nature with momentum and vitality, suggesting an intuition of an interconnected and dynamic universe.

For van Gogh's contemporaries, *Starry Night* was distressing for the unnatural liberties it took with its subject matter and for the intense emotion it expressed. Van Gogh's brother Theo was anxious about Vincent's poor mental health, and therefore praised (in his correspondence) van Gogh's more conventionally naturalist landscapes while passing over the more strikingly innovative work in silence. Even the painter himself worried that in the kind of abstraction in *Starry Night*—'stars too big, &c'—he had trodden on 'enchanted ground', taking a risk after a 'life of searching, of fighting hand-to-hand with reality'. Van Gogh died a year after painting *Starry Night*, having sold only a single painting in his lifetime. Yet after 71 of his paintings were exhibited at a retrospective in Paris in 1901, van Gogh would be recognized as the father of Expressionist painting and a key founder of modern art. Van Gogh's negative capability consisted in pursuing an original vision of the world and a radically new form of painting beyond the bounds of established sense and artistic practice.

Related to negative capability expressed in van Gogh's radical depiction of the night sky is the idea of defamiliarization. The Russian art theorist Viktor Shklovsky wrote of the 'defamiliarization' of the everyday in modern art, which it effected by diverging from expectations and prolonging the process of perception as the viewer faced an unfamiliar rendering of the world. Instigated by van Gogh among other innovators, modernist artists suspended what had been accepted as realist depiction. Expressionist painting highlighted a more intense and intuitive form of perception—with bold movement and explosive, sometimes incongruous, colour. Cubist painting sought not merely to fragment the look of the ordinary world but to reveal its availability to multiple perspectives. Surrealism challenged everyday appearances by blending depictions of recognizable things with illogical images to provoke raw feeling and dream-like associations.



Looking at things in an unfamiliar way may call our ordinary understanding of them—our cognitive habits—into question. Merleau-Ponty wrote that in modern painting it is towards a truer revelation of the world 'that its ordinary ties are broken'. But this departure from expectation is not merely a matter for art history or aesthetics. For with modern physics too the human intellect came to understand reality not as absolutely measurable in fixed terms but as defined by our ways of interacting with it. From a cultural perspective, the breakdown of appearances in modernist painting bears some analogy to a modern vision of reality itself.

In her acceptance speech for the Nobel Prize, the Polish poet laureate Wisława Szymborska paid tribute to the ideas of negative capability and defamiliarization in calling for an appreciation of astonishment. She argued that the task for the creative thinker is not merely to defeat the unknown, but to allow it to upset our usual expectations. Szymborska described how astonishment challenges the self-evident appearance of the ordinary world:

> What astonishment really exposes is that for all our acquisition of knowledge, all the comfortable familiarity we may have achieved, the world itself is anything but obvious.

Despite its divergence from a path of reasoning and fact, astonishment may be important for paradigm-shifting discovery even in the sciences. Szymborska cited Marie Curie and Isaac Newton as examples of scientists open to astonishment. In *The World as I See It* (1934), Einstein affirmed tolerance of the unknown or as he puts it, 'the mysterious'. For Einstein wonder at the mysterious 'is the fundamental emotion which stands at the cradle of true art and true science'. It befits a scientific outlook, he thought, to consider the highest achievements of the human mind as but 'an inkling of the marvelous structure of reality'.



Yet if the negative capability, defamiliarization, and astonishment associated with creative thinking suspend a need for rationalization, such dispositions may be in tension with curiosity, or the desire for knowledge. In their defence of rationality, some philosophers have regarded wonder with ambivalence, as did Descartes in his treatise *On the Passions of the Soul* (1649). He defined wonder as an effect of surprise on the soul that arises suddenly, provoked by novel and extraordinary phenomena. In a state of wonder we experience an interruption of previous expectation and a pause for inquisitive reflection. Descartes warned that excessive wonder may neutralize curiosity, or even 'entirely block or pervert the use of reason'. Yet wonder can motivate the pursuit of knowledge and so stimulate scientific study, as Descartes himself did in studying rainbows. Descartes exercised imaginative as well as rational cognition in demonstrating that the rainbow could be analysed through the principles of mathematics.

Wonder may initiate creativity, since it strikes us with difference from what we already know, our horizons of expectation thereby exposed, our cognitive habits for a moment suspended, our sense of possibilities awakened. As I discussed in *The Ecstatic Quotidian* (2007), artists and writers have noticed how the world as we experience it is vulnerable to such transformation. Rilke's poem 'Archaic Torso of Apollo' from his *New Poems* (1907) illustrates this kind of provocation. The poem describes an ancient Greek sculpture the poet came upon in the Louvre during a stay in Paris. Rilke's speaker feels existentially confronted by the fragmentary statue of the god Apollo, as it touches him with extraordinary power.

As the poem tells us, there is much the speaker cannot know about the original statue or the god it once represented. For it is but a fragment: 'we cannot know his legendary head', the poem begins. Yet, gazing at the artwork, the speaker is astonished by its sensuality, perfection, and vitality, and comes to feel gazed at in turn. In Rilke's famous final lines, the speaker feels to be directly addressed in the encounter: 'There is no place that does not see you. | You must change your life.' This unmistakably existential directive issues from the statue as if it opened a window to another world, a world that, gazing back upon the speaker, awaited a creative response. Rilke's poem of course does not tell the speaker, or the reader for that matter, what to do in changing a life, how to make the change, or even why. The provocation invites imagination in the contemplation of possibilities with which readers must engage if they are to answer the demand of the poem. The viewer of the Apollo statue and implicitly the reader of the poem are provoked not only to experience astonishment, but to creatively elaborate it.

While in Rilke's 'Archaic Torso of Apollo' this directive appears exceptional, a glance at some of the other experiences described in the *New Poems* suggests the latent wonder available to ordinary moments of life. We find the speaker of these poems fascinated by the rose window in a cathedral, a black cat, a blind woman making her way through a café, a panther at the Jardins du Luxembourg, an apple orchard viewed just after sunset, the glance of a dog from the perspective of which the speaker imagines its world taking shape. Just as creativity relies upon the mechanisms of everyday cognition, so too are we in everyday moments potentially vulnerable to wonder which may provoke a creative response.

Creativity not only contributes to human innovation but also has existential significance, and is an important ingredient in human happiness. Despite the stereotype of creative thinkers as suffering artists, contemporary psychological research shows that undertaking creative activities enhances feelings of well-being. This may be because through creativity we can stimulate what philosophers have called the 'feeling of life' in imagination's free play. Creativity reminds us of our own possibilities, and with its contribution to shaping our experience, promotes human flourishing.

We began this chapter by considering examples of creative expression that concretely manifest the metaphor of imaginative flight. We have seen that while inspiration sets creative moments apart from everyday experience, creativity draws from the same resources that subtend everyday thinking. Cognitive play describes diversion from habitual paths of thinking, connecting freedom and constraint, knowledge and openness to the not yet known. Negative capability and defamiliarization foster tolerance for the not yet fully understood, and wonder may stimulate shifts in ordinary thinking and spark our creative response. Creativity makes manifest and expressive the imagination that enlivens and liberates human thinking and supports our apprehension of a meaningful world.

# References

## Chapter 1: What is imagination?


Blaise Pascal, *Pensées* (New York: Dutton, 1958 [1669]), p. 82.

Samuel Johnson, *The History of Rasselas, Prince of Abissinia* (London: Cassell & Co., 1889 [1759]), p. 167.

Wallace Stevens, *The Necessary Angel: Essays on Reality and the Imagination* (New York: Alfred A. Knopf, 1951), p. 13.

Seamus Heaney, *The Redress of Poetry* (New York: Farrar, Straus and Giroux, 1995), pp. 3, 2.

Albert Einstein, 'What Life Means to Einstein', Interview with George Sylvester Vierack, *Saturday Evening Post* (October 1929), p. 117.

Albert Einstein and Leopold Infeld, *The Evolution of Physics* (London: The Scientific Book Club, 1938), p. 95.

Elizabeth Blackburn, 'Why Beauty is So Important to Us', *The New York Times*, Turning Points 2020: <https://www.nytimes.com/interactive/2019/12/07/opinion/elizabeth-blackburn-why-is-beauty-important.html>.

David Hume, *A Treatise of Human Nature*, ed. L. A. Selby-Bigge (Oxford: Clarendon, 1896 [1739]), p. 24.

Immanuel Kant, *Critique of Pure Reason*, trans. Paul Guyer and Alan W. Wood (Cambridge: Cambridge University Press, 1998 [1781]), A141:B180–1.

Gilbert Ryle, *The Concept of Mind* (New York: Routledge, 2009 [1949]), pp. 224–5.

Jean-Paul Sartre, *The Imaginary: A Phenomenological Psychology of Imagination*, trans. Jonathan Webber (London and New York: Routledge, 2004 [1940]).

## Chapter 2: Imagination in human evolution

For background on human cognitive evolution see Steven Mithen, 'The Evolution of Imagination: An Archeological Perspective', *Substance*, issue 94/95 vol. 30 nos 1–2 (2001), 28–54; Robin Dunbar, *The Human Story: A New History of Mankind's Evolution* (London: Faber and Faber, 2005); Peter Gärdenfors, *How Homo Became Sapiens: On the Evolution of Thinking* (Oxford: Oxford University Press, 2003); R. Dale Guthrie, *The Nature of Paleolithic Art* (Chicago: University of Chicago Press, 2005); Christopher Collins, *Paleopoetics: The Evolution of the Preliterate Imagination* (New York: Columbia University Press, 2013); and chapter 2 of Jennifer Gosetti-Ferencei, *The Life of Imagination: Revealing and Making the World* (New York: Columbia University Press, 2018).

D. W. Winnicott, *Playing and Reality* (London: Tavistock, 1971), p. 67.

Paul L. Harris, *The Work of Imagination* (Oxford: Blackwell, 2000).

Maurice Merleau-Ponty, *The World of Perception*, trans. Oliver Davis (London and New York: Routledge, 2004), p. 74.

For background on animal imagining see Anthony D. Pellegrini and Peter K. Smith, eds, *The Nature of Play: Great Apes and Humans* (New York: Guilford Press, 2005); and Robert W. Mitchell, *Pretending and Imagination in Animals and Children* (Cambridge: Cambridge University Press, 2011).

## Chapter 3: From divine madness to cognitive power

Plato, *Republic, vols. I and II*, trans. Paul Shorey, Loeb Classical Library (Cambridge, Mass. and London: Harvard University Press and William Heinemann, 1942). Citations are from 598b, 601b–c, 603a.

Plato, *Statesman, Philebus, Ion*, trans. Harold North Fowler, Loeb Classical Library (Cambridge, Mass. and London: Harvard University Press and William Heinemann, 1925). Citations are from *Philebus*, 39b, 39e.

Aristotle, *On the Soul, Parva Naturalia, On Breath*, trans. W. S. Hett, Loeb Classical Library (Cambridge, Mass.: Harvard University Press, 2000). Citations are from *On the Soul*, 428a2–3, 428a16, 427b20, 429a4, 431a17–18, 431b 4–5, 431b6–9.

Miguel de Montaigne, *Essays in Ten Volumes*, trans. Charles Colton, ed. William C. Hazlett (New York: Edwin C. Hill, 1910 [1580]), citation vol. 1 p. 214.

William Shakespeare, *The Complete Works*, 2nd edition, ed. John Jowett et al. (Oxford: Oxford University Press, 2005). Citations are from *A Midsummer Night's Dream*, Act I Scene 5, and *Richard II*, Act I Scene 3.
René Descartes, *Discourse on Method and Meditations on First Philosophy*, trans. Donald A. Cress (Indianapolis: Hackett, 1998 [1637/1641]), pp. 19, 22, 28, 22.
David Hume, *Enquiries Concerning Human Understanding*, ed. Tom L. Beauchamp (Oxford: Oxford University Press, 1999 [1748]), p. 124.
Hume, *A Treatise of Human Nature*, p. 259.

## Chapter 4: The productive and aesthetic imagination

Immanuel Kant, *Anthropology from a Pragmatic Point of View*, ed. Robert B. Louden (Cambridge: Cambridge University Press, 2006 [1798]), p. 7:153.
Kant, *Critique of Pure Reason*, p. A120.
Immanuel Kant, *Critique of Judgment*, trans. Werner S. Pluhar (Indianapolis: Hackett, 1987 [1790]), pp. 242, 314, 315.
Edmund Burke, *A Philosophical Enquiry into the Origin of Our Ideas of the Sublime and the Beautiful*, ed. J. T. Boulton (London: Routledge and Kegan Paul, 1958 [1757]), p. 57.
Kant, *Critique of Judgment*, pp. 255, 259, 262.
Jean-François Lyotard, *Lessons on the Analytic of the Sublime*, trans. Elizabeth Rottenberg (Stanford, Calif.: Stanford University Press, 1994).
Samuel Taylor Coleridge, *Biographia Literaria, The Collected Works of Samuel Taylor Coleridge vol. 7*, ed. James Engell and W. Jackson Bate (Princeton: Princeton University Press 1985 [1817]), p. 295.
Samuel Taylor Coleridge, *Letters vol. I*, ed. Earl Leslie Griggs (Oxford: Clarendon, 1959), p. 354.
William Wordsworth, *The Prelude, 1799, 1805, 1850: Authoritative Texts, Context and Reception, Recent Critical Essays*, ed. Jonathan Wordsworth, M. H. Abrams, and Stephen Gill (London and New York: Norton, 1979). Citation is from the 1799 version, lines 121–9.
Friedrich Hölderlin, *Hyperion and Selected Poems*, ed. Eric L. Santer (New York: Continuum, 1990), p. 189.
Friedrich Schlegel, *Philosophical Fragments*, trans. Peter Firchow (Minneapolis and London: University of Minnesota Press, 1991), pp. 70–1, 39, 95.

Friedrich Nietzsche, *The Birth of Tragedy: Out of the Spirit of Music*, trans. Shaun Whiteside (London and New York: Penguin Classics, 1993), p. 18.
Friedrich Nietzsche, 'On Truth and Lies in a Nonmoral Sense', in *Philosophy and Truth: Selections from Nietzsche's Notebooks of the Early 1870s*, ed. and trans. Daniel Breazeale (Amherst, NY: Humanity Books, 1999), p. 86.
Friedrich Nietzsche, *Philosophy in the Tragic Age of the Greeks*, trans. Marianne Cowan (Washington, DC: Regnery, 1962), p. 40.

## Chapter 5: The augmentation of reality

Ludwig Wittgenstein, *Philosophical Investigations*, trans. P. M. S. Hacker and Joachim Schulte (Oxford: Blackwell, 2009 [1953]), p. 193.
P. F. Strawson, 'Imagination and Perception', in *Freedom and Resentment and Other Essays* (New York: Routledge, 2008 [1974]), p. 58.
Wittgenstein, *Philosophical Investigations*, pp. 200, 205.
Stephen. M. Kosslyn, *Image and Mind* (Cambridge, Mass.: Harvard University Press, 1980).
Edward S. Casey, *Imagining: A Phenomenological Study*, 2nd edition (Bloomington: Indiana University Press, 2000).
William James, *Principles of Psychology* (New York: Henry Holt and Company, 1890/1950), p. 58.
Vladimir Nabokov, *Lectures on Russian Literature* (New York: Harcourt, 1981).
William H. Gass, *Fiction and the Figures of Life* (New York: Albert Knopf, 1970).
Maurice Merleau-Ponty, 'Eye and Mind', in *The Merleau-Ponty Aesthetics Reader*, ed. Galen A. Johnson (Evanston, Ill.: Northwestern University Press, 1993).
Maurice Merleau-Ponty, *The Visible and the Invisible, Followed by Working Notes*, trans. Alphonso Lingus (Evanston, Ill.: Northwestern University Press, 1968).
Jean-Paul Sartre, *Being and Nothingness*, trans. Hazel Barnes (New York: Washington Square, 1992 [1943]), p. 488.
Sartre, *The Imaginary*, pp. 183, 236.
Paul Ricoeur, 'The Narrative Function', in John B. Thompson, ed., *Paul Ricoeur: Hermeneutics and the Human Sciences* (Cambridge: Cambridge University Press, 1979), p. 292.
Stevens, *The Necessary Angel*, p. 65.

Benedict Anderson, *Imagined Communities* (New York: Verso Books, 2006 [1983]).
Hannah Arendt, *The Origins of Totalitarianism* (New York: Harcourt Brace, 1951).
François Jacob, 'Imagination in Art and in Science', trans. Tracy Ryan, *The Kenyon Review* New Series 23:2 (Spring 2001), 113–21, p. 120.

## Chapter 6: Creativity from invention to wonder

Plato, from *Ion* in *Statesman, Philebus, Ion*, p. 534b.
Gosetti-Ferencei, *The Life of Imagination*, p. 218.
Kant, *Critique of Judgment*, pp. 312–13, 308.
John Dewey, *Art as Experience* (New York: Capricorn Books, 1934), p. 15.
Arthur Koestler, *The Act of Creation*, p. 231.
Gilles Fauconnier and Mark Turner, *The Way We Think: Conceptual Blending and the Mind's Hidden Complexities* (New York: Basic Books, 2002), p. 18.
Charles Baudelaire, *Les Fleurs du mal/Flowers of Evil*, revised, edited, trans. John E. Tidball (Bishopston Editions, 2016), p. 429.
Charles Baudelaire, from 'The Salon of 1859', in *The Mirror of Art: Critical Studies*, trans. and ed. Jonathan Mayne (New York: Doubleday 1956), p. 241.
Robert Frost, *Collected Prose of Robert Frost*, ed. Mark Richardson (Cambridge: Belknap, 2007), pp. 131, 132, 131.
Igor Stravinsky, *The Poetics of Music in the Form of Six Lessons*, trans. Arthur Knodel and Ingolf Dahl (Cambridge, Mass.: Harvard University Press, 1947 [1942]), pp. 63, 64–5.
Toni Morrison, *The Source of Self-Regard: Selected Essays, Speeches, and Meditations* (New York: Knopf, 2019), p. 320.
Friedrich Schiller, *On the Aesthetic Education of Man in a Series of Letters*, ed. and trans. Elizabeth M. Wilkinson and L. A. Willoughby (Oxford: Clarendon Press, 1967 [1774–75]), p. 107.
Hans-Georg Gadamer, *Truth and Method*, trans. Joel Weisenheimer and Donald G. Marshall (London: Bloomsbury Academic, 2013).
John Keats, in a letter to his brothers of 1817, in *The Complete Poetical Works and Letters of John Keats, Cambridge Edition* (New York: Houghton, Mifflin and Company, 1899), p. 277.
Maurice Merleau-Ponty, *Signs*, trans. Richard McCleary (Evanston, Ill.: Northwestern University Press, 1964), pp. 53, 56.

Vincent van Gogh 'Letter to Emile Bernard', 26 November 1889, in *Painted with Words: Letters to Emile Bernard*, ed. Leo Jansen, Hans Luijten, and Nienke Bakker (New York: The Morgan Library and Amsterdam: Van Gogh Museum, 2007), pp. 339–40.

Viktor Shklovsky, 'Art as Technique', in *Russian Formalist Criticism: Four Essays*, ed. Lee T. Lemon and Marion J. Reiss (Lincoln: University of Nebraska Press, 1965), pp. 3–24.

Wisława Szymborska, Nobel Lecture. NobelPrize.org. Nobel Prize Outreach AB 2022. Tue. 19 July 2022. <https://www.nobelprize.org/prizes/literature/1996/szymborska/lecture/>.

Albert Einstein, *The World as I See It*, trans. Alan Harris (London: John Lane, 1935), pp. 4–5.

René Descartes, *The Passions of the Soul*, trans. Stephen H. Voss (Indianapolis/Cambridge: Hackett Publishing, 1989), p. 59.

Rainer Maria Rilke, 'Archaic Torso of Apollo', in *New Poems, Bilingual Edition*, trans. Stephen Mitchell (New York: Knopf Doubleday, 2013).

# Further reading


Brann, Eva T. H., *The World of the Imagination: Sum and Substance* (Savage, Md: Rowman & Littlefield, 1991).

Casey, Edward S., *Imagining: A Phenomenological Study*, 2nd edition (Bloomington: Indiana University Press, 2000).

Collins, Christopher, *Neopoetics: Evolution of the Literate Imagination* (New York: Columbia University Press, 2016).

Currie, Gregory, and Ian Ravenscroft, *Recreative Minds: Imagination in Philosophy and Psychology* (Oxford: Oxford University Press, 2002).

Edelman, Gerald, and G. Tononi, *A Universe of Consciousness: How Matter Becomes Imagination* (New York: Basic Books, 2000).

Fauconnier, Gilles, and Mark Turner, *The Way We Think: Conceptual Blending and the Mind's Hidden Complexities* (New York: Basic Books, 2002).

Gosetti-Ferencei, Jennifer Anna, *The Ecstatic Quotidian: Phenomenological Sightings in Modern Art and Literature* (University Park, Pa: The Pennsylvania State University Press, 2007).

Gosetti-Ferencei, Jennifer Anna, *The Life of Imagination: Revealing and Making the World* (New York: Columbia University Press, 2018).

Hannay, Alastair, *Mental Images: A Defence* (Abingdon and New York: Routledge, 2002).

Hofstadter, Douglas, and Emmanuel Sander, *Surfaces and Essences: Analogy as the Fuel and Fire of Thinking* (New York: Basic Books, 2013).

Husserl, Edmund, *Phantasy, Image Consciousness, and Memory (1898–1925)*, trans. John Brough (Dordrecht: Springer Academic Publishers, 2005).

Iser, Wolfgang, *The Fictive and the Imaginary: Charting Literary Anthropology* (Baltimore: The Johns Hopkins University Press, 1993).

Johnson, Mark, *The Body in the Mind: The Bodily Basis of Meaning, Imagination, and Reason* (Chicago: University of Chicago Press, 1990).

Kandel, Eric, *Reductionism in Art and Brain Science: Bridging the Two Cultures* (New York: Columbia University Press, 2016).

Kearney, Richard, *Poetics of Imagining: Modern to Post-Modern* (New York: Fordham University Press, 1998).

Kind, Amy, and Peter Kung, eds, *Knowledge through Imagination* (Oxford: Oxford University Press, 2016).

Kind, Amy, ed., *The Routledge Handbook of Philosophy of Imagination* (London and New York: Routledge, 2016).

Koestler, Arthur, *The Act of Creation* (London and New York: Penguin, 1964).

Kosslyn, Stephen M., William L. Thompson, and Giorgio Ganis, *The Case for Mental Imagery* (Oxford: Oxford University Press, 2006).

Lakoff, George, and Mark Johnson, *Metaphors We Live By* (Chicago: University of Chicago Press, 1980).

Lakoff, George, and Mark Johnson, *Philosophy in the Flesh: The Embodied Mind and Its Challenge to Western Thought* (New York: Basic Books, 1999).

Lennon, Kathleen, *Imagination and the Imaginary* (New York: Routledge, 2015).

Lewis-Williams, D., *The Mind in the Cave: Consciousness and the Origin of Art* (London: Thames & Hudson, 2002).

Lyons, John D., *Before Imagination: Embodied Thought from Montaigne to Rousseau* (Stanford, Calif.: Stanford University Press, 2005).

Merleau-Ponty, Maurice, *The Merleau-Ponty Aesthetics Reader*, ed. Galen A. Johnson (Evanston, Ill.: Northwestern University Press, 1993).

Modell, Arnold H., *Imagination and the Meaningful Brain* (Cambridge, Mass.: MIT Press, 2003).

Nichols, Shaun, ed., *The Architecture of Imagination: New Essays on Pretence, Possibility, and Fiction* (Oxford: Oxford University Press, 2006).

Paul, Elliot Samuel, and Scott Barry Kaufman, eds, *The Philosophy of Creativity: New Essays* (Oxford: Oxford University Press, 2014).
Ricoeur, Paul, *The Rule of Metaphor* (Chicago: Chicago University Press, 1977).
Ricoeur, Paul, *A Ricoeur Reader: Reflection and Imagination*, ed. Mario J. Valdés (Toronto: University of Toronto Press, 1991, reprinted 2012).
Sartre, Jean-Paul, *The Imagination: A Psychological Critique*, trans. Forrest Williams (Ann Arbor: University of Michigan, 1962).
Sartre, Jean-Paul, *What is Literature? and Other Essays* (Cambridge, Mass.: Harvard University Press, 1988).
Sartre, Jean-Paul, *The Imaginary: A Phenomenological Psychology of Imagination*, trans. Jonathan Webber (London and New York: Routledge, 2004). First published 1940.
Scarry, Elaine, *Dreaming by the Book: On Literary Imagining* (Princeton: Princeton University Press, 1999).
Schultz, Alexander M., *Mind's World: Imagination and Subjectivity from Descartes to Romanticism* (Seattle: University of Washington Press, 2009).
Scruton, Roger, *Art and Imagination* (London: Methuen, 1970).
Sepper, Dennis L., *Descartes's Imagination: Proportion, Images, and the Activity of Thinking* (Berkeley and Los Angeles: University of California Press, 1996).
Sternberg, Robert J., *Handbook of Creativity* (Cambridge: Cambridge University Press, 2008).
Taylor, Marjorie, ed., *Oxford Handbook of the Development of Imagination* (Oxford: Oxford University Press, 2013).
Turner, Mark, *The Literary Mind* (Oxford: Oxford University Press, 1997).
Turner, Mark, ed., *The Artful Mind: Cognitive Science and the Riddle of Human Creativity* (New York: Oxford University Press, 2006).
Turner, Mark, and Gilles Fauconnier, 'A Mechanism of Creativity', *Poetics Today* 20:3 (1999).
Warnock, Mary, 'Imagination in Sartre', *British Journal of Aesthetics* 10:4 (1970), 323–36.
Warnock, Mary, *Imagination* (Berkeley and Los Angeles: University of California Press, 1976).
Weisburg, Robert W., *Creativity: Beyond the Myth of Genius* (Hoboken, NJ: Wiley, 2006).
White, Alan R., *The Language of Imagination* (Oxford: Blackwell, 1990).

# Index

For the benefit of digital users, indexed terms that span two pages (e.g., 52–53) may, on occasion, appear on only one of those pages.

## D



## E



## F



## G



## H



## I

# DREAMING

## A Very Short Introduction

J. Allan Hobson

What is dreaming and what causes it? Why are dreams so strange and often hard to remember?

In this *Very Short Introduction*, J. Allan Hobson provides a new and increasingly complete picture of how dreaming is created by the brain. Hobson offers possible answers to long-held questions on activation, function, and the interpretation of dreams, and reveals how dreaming maintains and develops the mind. As well as investigating the relationship between dreaming, learning, memory, and consciousness, Hobson investigates his own dreams to illustrate and explain some of the fascinating discoveries of modern sleep science.

www.oup.com/vsi

# MEMORY

## A Very Short Introduction

Michael J. Benton

Why do we remember events from our childhood as if they happened yesterday, but not what we did last week? Why does our memory seem to work well sometimes and not others? What happens when it goes wrong? Can memory be improved or manipulated, by psychological techniques or even 'brain implants'? How does memory grow and change as we age? And what of so-called 'recovered' memories? This book brings together the latest research in neuroscience and psychology, and weaves in case-studies, anecdotes, and even literature and philosophy, to address these and many other important questions about the science of memory - how it works, and why we can't live without it.

www.oup.com/vsi

# BEAUTY

## A Very Short Introduction

Roger Scruton

In this *Very Short Introduction* the renowned philosopher Roger Scruton explores the concept of beauty, asking what makes an object - either in art, in nature, or the human form - beautiful, and examining how we can compare differing judgements of beauty when it is evident all around us that our tastes vary so widely. Is there a right judgement to be made about beauty? Is it right to say there is more beauty in a classical temple than a concrete office block, more in a Rembrandt than in last year's Turner Prize winner? Forthright and thought-provoking, and as accessible as it is intellectually rigorous, this introduction to the philosophy of beauty draws conclusions that some may find controversial, but, as Scruton shows, help us to find greater sense of meaning in the beautiful objects that fill our lives.

A fascinating book, which I heartily recommend.

**Brya Wilson, Readers Digest**

# FAIRY TALE

## A Very Short Introduction

Marina Warner

From wicked queens to goblins and giants, glass slippers to poisoned apples, the characters and images of fairy tales have cast a spell over readers for centuries. Few forms of literature have greater power to enchant us and rekindle our imagination than a fairy tale.

In this *Very Short Introduction*, Marina Warner digs into a rich hoard of fairy tales in all their brilliant and fantastical variations, in order to define a genre and evaluate a literary form that keeps shifting through time and history. Drawing on a glittering array of examples, from classics such as Red Riding Hood, Cinderella, and The Sleeping Beauty, to modern-day realizations including Walt Disney's *Snow White*, Warner forms a persuasive case for fairy tale as a crucial repository of human understanding and culture.

www.oup.com/vsi

# Chaos

## A Very Short Introduction

Leonard Smith

Our growing understanding of Chaos Theory is having fascinating applications in the real world - from technology to global warming, politics, human behaviour, and even gambling on the stock market. Leonard Smith shows that we all have an intuitive understanding of chaotic systems. He uses accessible maths and physics (replacing complex equations with simple examples like pendulums, railway lines, and tossing coins) to explain the theory, and points to numerous examples in philosophy and literature (Edgar Allen Poe, Chang-Tzu, Arthur Conan Doyle) that illuminate the problems. The beauty of fractal patterns and their relation to chaos, as well as the history of chaos, and its uses in the real world and implications for the philosophy of science are all discussed in this *Very Short Introduction.*

> '. . . Chaos . . . will give you the clearest (but not too painful idea) of the maths involved . . . There's a lot packed into this little book, and for such a technical exploration it's surprisingly readable and enjoyable - I really wanted to keep turning the pages. Smith also has some excellent words of wisdom about common misunderstandings of chaos theory . . .'
>
> **popularscience.co.uk**

# COMEDY

## A Very Short Introduction

Matthew Bevis

What is humour, and how may it be used (or abused)? When do we laugh, and why? What is it that writers and speakers enjoy—or risk—when they tell a joke, indulge in bathos, talk nonsense, or encourage irony?

This *Very Short Introduction* considers comedy not only as a literary genre, but also as a broader impulse at work in many other historical and contemporary forms of satire, parody, and play. Matthew Bevis takes us through the history of comedy, from the work of John Gay and Richard Sheridan in the eighteenth century to twentieth-century dramatists like Ionesco, Brecht and Cocteau, up to present day interpretations of comedy, such as Charlie Kaufman's *Being John Malkovich* and Channel 4's *Peep Show.*

www.oup.com/vsi

# CONSCIENCE

## A Very Short Introduction

Paul Strohm

In the West conscience has been relied upon for two thousand years as a judgement that distinguishes right from wrong. It has effortlessly moved through every period division and timeline between the ancient, medieval, and modern. The Romans identified it, the early Christians appropriated it, and Reformation Protestants and loyal Catholics relied upon its advice and admonition. Today it is embraced with equal conviction by non-religious and religious alike. Considering its deep historical roots and exploring what it has meant to successive generations, Paul Strohm highlights why this particularly European concept deserves its reputation as 'one of the prouder Western contributions to human rights and human dignity throughout the world.

www.oup.com/vsi

# FASHION
## A Very Short Introduction
Rebecca Arnold

Fashion is a dynamic global industry that plays an important role in the economic, political, cultural, and social lives of an international audience. It spans high art and popular culture, and plays a significant role in material and visual culture. This book introduces fashion's myriad influences and manifestations. Fashion is explored as a creative force, a business, and a means of communication. From Karl Lagerfeld's creative reinventions of Chanel's iconic style to the multicultural reference points of Indian designer Manish Arora, from the spectacular fashion shows held in nineteenth century department stores to the mix-and-match styles of Japanese youth, the book examines the ways that fashion both reflects and shapes contemporary culture.

'Her fascinating little book makes a good framework for independent study and has a very useful bibliography.'

**Philippa Stockley, Times Literary Supplement**

www.oup.com/vsi

# GENIUS

## A Very Short Introduction

Andrew Robinson

Genius is highly individual and unique, of course, yet it shares a compelling, inevitable quality for professionals and the general public alike. Darwin's ideas are still required reading for every working biologist; they continue to generate fresh thinking and experiments around the world. So do Einstein's theories among physicists. Shakespeare's plays and Mozart's melodies and harmonies continue to move people in languages and cultures far removed from their native England and Austria. Contemporary 'geniuses' may come and go, but the idea of genius will not let go of us. Genius is the name we give to a quality of work that transcends fashion, celebrity, fame, and reputation: the opposite of a period piece. Somehow, genius abolishes both the time and the place of its origin.

www.oup.com/vsi

# LOVE
## A Very Short Introduction
Ronald de Sousa

Erotic love has been celebrated in art and poetry as life's most rewarding and exalting experience, worth living and dying for and bringing out the best in ourselves. *And yet it has excused, and even been thought to justify, the most reprehensible crimes. Why should this be?*

This *Very Short Introduction* explores this and other puzzling questions. Ronald de Sousa considers some of the many paradoxes created by love, looking at the different kinds of love (affections, affiliation, *philia*, *storage*, and *agape*) with a focus on *eros*, or romantic love. He considers whether our conventional beliefs about love and sex are deeply irrational and argues that alternative conceptions of love and sex, although hard to formulate and live by, may be worth striving for.

www.oup.com/vsi